The Breakfast Club

The Breakfast Club is a quintessential teen film. This book analyzes how multiple factors coalesced to solidify the status of *The Breakfast Club* as one of the most emblematic films of the 1980s and one of the most definitive teen films of the genre. The film brings together genre-defining elements – the conflicts between generations and peer pressure, archetypical characters and breaking down stereotypes, the celebration and survival of adolescence, and the importance of this time in life on the coming-of-age process – and became a significant moment for John Hughes as an auteur and for teen films in the 1980s. More than just embodying these elements of the genre, filmmaker Hughes and the Brat Pack stars helped introduce and popularize multiple generic features that would come to be expected with the teen film formula. The content of the film combined with its context of production in the middle of a boom in teen filmmaking in Hollywood. Meanwhile, the marketing that focused on contemporary music, peer group dynamics, and oppositions between Generation X and baby boomers, merged with an enthusiastic reception by youth audiences. Its endurance speaks to the way the film's level of importance as a critical, commercial, and influential film with tremendous impact has grown since its initial debut.

Elissa H. Nelson is an Assistant Professor in the Department of Communication Arts and Sciences at Bronx Community College, CUNY. She has published work on 1980s Hollywood, digital distribution, and teen films. Her current research focuses on media industries, genre, soundtracks, and representations of youth.

Cinema and Youth Cultures

Series Editors: Siân Lincoln and Yannis Tzioumakis

Cinema and Youth Cultures engages with well-known youth films from American cinema as well the cinemas of other countries. Using a variety of methodological and critical approaches the series volumes provide informed accounts of how young people have been represented in film, while also exploring the ways in which young people engage with films made for and about them. In doing this, the Cinema and Youth Cultures series contributes to important and long-standing debates about youth cultures, how these are mobilized and articulated in influential film texts, and the impact that these texts have had on popular culture at large.

Boyhood
Timothy Shary

Easy A
Betty Kaklamanidou

The Hunger Games
Catherine Driscoll and Alexandra Heatwole

L'Auberge Espagnole
Ben McCann

The Virgin Suicides
Justin Wyatt

The Breakfast Club
John Hughes, Hollywood, and the Golden Age of the Teen Film
Elissa H. Nelson

For more information about this series, please visit: www.routledge.com/ Cinema-and-Youth-Cultures/book-series/CYC

The Breakfast Club

John Hughes, Hollywood, and the Golden Age of the Teen Film

Elissa H. Nelson

Frontispiece: Poster/One-Sheet for *The Breakfast Club*

Source: photographed by Annie Leibovitz. Courtesy of Universal/Kobal/REX/Shutterstock

Routledge
Taylor & Francis Group

LONDON AND NEW YORK

First published 2019
by Routledge
2 Park Square, Milton Park, Abingdon, Oxon OX14 4RN

and by Routledge
605 Third Avenue, New York, NY 10017

First issued in paperback 2021

Routledge is an imprint of the Taylor & Francis Group, an informa business

British Library Cataloguing-in-Publication Data
A catalogue record for this book is available from the British Library

Library of Congress Cataloging-in-Publication Data
Names: Nelson, Elissa H., author.
Title: The Breakfast Club: John Hughes, Hollywood, and the golden
    age of the teen film / Elissa H. Nelson.
Description: London ; New York : Routledge, 2019. | Series: Cinema
    and youth cultures ; 8 | Includes bibliographical references.
Identifiers: LCCN 2018058372 (print) | LCCN 2019010906 (ebook) |
    ISBN 9781315545486 (ebook) | ISBN 9781138681927 (hardback :
    alk. paper) | ISBN 9781315545486 (ebk)
Subjects: LCSH: Breakfast club (Motion picture) | Teen films—History
    and criticism. | Teenagers in motion pictures.
Classification: LCC PN1997.B72285 (ebook) | LCC PN1997.B72285 N45
    2019 (print) | DDC 791.43/65235—dc23
LC record available at https://lccn.loc.gov/2018058372

ISBN 13: 978-0-367-78807-0 (pbk)
ISBN 13: 978-1-138-68192-7 (hbk)

Typeset in Times New Roman
by Apex CoVantage, LLC

For my parents

Contents

Figures

Series editors' introduction

Despite the high visibility of youth films in the global media marketplace, especially since the 1980s when Conglomerate Hollywood realized that such films were not only strong box-office performers but also the starting point for ancillary sales in other media markets as well as for franchise building, academic studies that focused specifically on such films were slow to materialize. Arguably the most important factor behind academia's reluctance to engage with youth films was a (then) widespread perception within the Film and Media Studies communities that such films held little cultural value and significance and therefore were not worthy of serious scholarly research and examination. Just like the young subjects they represented, whose interests and cultural practices have been routinely deemed transitional and transitory, so were the films that represented them perceived as fleeting and easily digestible, destined to be forgotten quickly, as soon as the next youth film arrived in cinema screens a week later.

Under these circumstances, and despite a small number of pioneering studies in the 1980s and early 1990s, the field of 'youth film studies' did not really start blossoming and attracting significant scholarly attention until the 2000s and in combination with similar developments in cognate areas such as 'girl studies.' However, because of the paucity of material in the previous decades, the majority of these new studies in the 2000s focused primarily on charting the field and therefore steered clear of long, in-depth examinations of youth films or were exemplified by edited collections that chose particular films to highlight certain issues to the detriment of others. In other words, despite providing often wonderfully rich accounts of youth cultures as these have been captured by key films, these studies could not have possibly dedicated sufficient space to engage with more than just a few key aspects of youth films.

In more recent (post-2010) years, a number of academic studies started delimiting their focus and therefore providing more space for in-depth examinations of key types of youth films, such as slasher films and biker films, or examining youth films in particular historical periods. From that point on, it was a matter of time before the first publications that focused exclusively on key youth films from a number of perspectives would appear (*Mamma Mia! The Movie*, *Twilight*, and *Dirty Dancing* are among the first films to receive this treatment). Conceived primarily as edited collections, these studies provided a multifaceted analysis of these films, focusing on such issues as the politics of representing youth, the stylistic and narrative choices that characterize these films and the extent to which they are representative of a youth cinema, the ways these films address their audiences, the ways youth audiences engage with these films, the films' industrial location, and other relevant issues.

It is within this increasingly maturing and expanding academic environment that the **Cinema and Youth Cultures** volumes arrive, aiming to consolidate existing knowledge, provide new perspectives, apply innovative methodological approaches, offer sustained and in-depth analyses of key films and therefore become the 'go-to' resource for students and scholars interested in theoretically informed, authoritative accounts of youth cultures in film. As editors, we have tried to be as inclusive as possible in our selection of key examples of youth films by commissioning volumes on films that span the history of cinema, including the silent film era; portray contemporary youth cultures as well as ones associated with particular historical periods; represent examples of mainstream and independent cinema; originate in American cinema and the cinemas of other nations; attracted significant critical attention and commercial success during their initial release; and were 'rediscovered' after an unpromising initial critical reception. Together, these volumes will advance youth film studies while also being able to offer extremely detailed examinations of films that are now considered significant contributions to cinema and our cultural life more broadly.

We hope readers will enjoy the series.

Siân Lincoln and Yannis Tzioumakis
Cinema and Youth Cultures Series Editors

Acknowledgments

Yannis Tzioumakis and Siân Lincoln deserve much thanks and praise for helping me with this book. I have been fortunate to know Yannis for almost a decade, and he constantly impresses me with his enthusiasm, encouragement, keen eye, and kindness; I am so grateful for his and Siân's stewardship. Gratitude also goes to Thomas Schatz and Karin Wilkins; their insightful guidance still influences me.

Thanks foremost go to my parents, William and Josette, who have been so supportive, and also to my invaluable and instrumental siblings, extended family, friends, colleagues, and students, especially Kara King, Lucylla Baynes, Christian Harris, and Kevin Bozelka. Steven Dickstein holds my great appreciation and awe for being a mensch and then some.

Introduction

The Breakfast Club and the golden age of the teen film

Five teenagers being forced to sit in a library for nine hours of detention hardly seems like an exciting premise for one of the most exemplary films of the teen film genre or for one of the most memorable films from the 1980s. But immediately upon hearing the bare-bones plot description, recollections are triggered: Bender pumping his fist in the air as he walks across the field with the familiar chords and lyrics of 'Don't You (Forget About Me)' playing over the still frame, the voiceover of Brian reading an essay giving character types instead of names, Allison shaking dandruff from her hair to make snowflakes on her drawing, five high schoolers sitting apart from one another in the cavernous library at the beginning and then all dancing together on the furniture by the end. That *The Breakfast Club* (Hughes 1985) can be so vividly recalled even thirty-plus years after its release is a testament to its power and lasting significance. It is an indication that the film was able to touch on something enduring about adolescence, about where people fit into social groups, and about the process of growing up while trying to stay true to the values of youth that all still ring true.

The Breakfast Club is arguably one of the most canonical teen films produced during the 1980s, the most prolific period of teen filmmaking in the US. As such, this book focuses on how elements of the teen film genre crystalized during the decade, how *The Breakfast Club* became a defining film of the era through its emphasis on character types and generational conflict, and how the particular talent assembled was able to give voice to a poignant and influential portrait of youth culture. Importantly, this study looks at both the content of the film as well as its context of production, i.e., at the textual elements that comprise the film and at what was happening in the Hollywood industry and the country at large at the time the film was made.

The film itself focuses predominantly on teen characters during the 1980s, a time when the Hollywood film industry was gearing more and more of its products to the youth demographic. But more than just featuring a cast of popular Brat Pack actors, the film spoke to the generation coming of age at the time with a story that got to the heart of the conflict between adults and young adults, that understood both the camaraderie and the pressures of peer groups, and that unabashedly dealt with teenagers as real people with real problems. With writer and director John Hughes's unique voice at the helm, the film capitalized on a culture already targeting the youth market, and by telling its tale from a youth perspective, it was able to leave a lasting impression on both contemporary and present-day audiences.

From a Hollywood industrial perspective, the film was produced at an ideal time. The 1980s witnessed a surge of teen film production that had not been seen in Hollywood since the 1950s. In terms of sheer numbers, teen films made up approximately one of every ten films produced throughout the decade and an average of one of every five to six of the top fifty grossing films per year (Nelson 2011: 2). This focus on teen film production came at a time when the youth market was increasing its buying power, when the youth demographic group had more leisure time and more disposable income to spend as a result of recent upswings in the US economy.

The 1980s also saw significant changes in the Hollywood film industry. While teens had more money to spend, there were fears that box-office attendance would start to plummet because of the new competing technologies of cable and home video. One of the consistent strategies Hollywood uses to combat audience attrition, especially when there is competition from new media (Nelson 2017: 126), is producing films with specific appeal to teen audiences, who have been some of the most reliable moviegoers since the 1950s. Teen films were made during the 1980s with this specific intent in mind.

The Breakfast Club capitalized not just on the teen film production trend but also on the talent that was available at the time. Indeed, the decade presented a confluence of circumstances conducive to the spate of teen films produced. The Brat Pack, a group of young actors who frequently worked together and were becoming stars in their own rights, started to gain in popularity. Molly Ringwald, Anthony Michael Hall, Emilio Estevez, Judd Nelson, and Ally Sheedy starred in *The Breakfast Club*, and within a few years of each other, also starred in films like *Sixteen Candles* (Hughes 1984) and *St. Elmo's Fire* (Schumacher 1985). The 1980s was the first time there was a somewhat cohesive group of young talent frequently working together. They had both the star power to raise the awareness and marketability of films and the presence, by very nature of their young age, to signify the importance of the teen trend in filmmaking (see Figure 0.1).

While the talent was available in terms of casting, the importance of writer and director John Hughes must be noted as well. Hughes was adamant about directing *The Breakfast Club*, and even though he had limited experience as a director, he was able to do so because of its small budget. However, he was also garnering a reputation in Hollywood because of

Figure 0.1 The Breakfast Club publicity still; five popular young actors in front of
lockers indicate a teen film.

previous work and because of scripts in the production pipeline. His was the
talent as the writer and/or director behind films such as *Sixteen Candles*, *Weird
Science* (Hughes 1985), *Ferris Bueller's Day Off* (Hughes 1986), *Pretty
in Pink* (Deutch 1986), and *Some Kind of Wonderful* (Deutch 1987). In the
middle of making this streak of popular teen films, he was already being
called an auteur (O'Connor 1986), someone with a distinct and recognizable
filmmaking style. Instead of writing from an adult point of view, Hughes
tried to approach teens and their stories from the perspective of youth themselves, seemingly more successfully than anyone had previously done, and

repeated formal and thematic elements, such as delving into the intricacies of teen social groupings, which he continually explored in ways that resonated with audiences. When Hughes passed away suddenly in 2009 at the age of 59, an article in *Entertainment Weekly* summed up his contribution powerfully and astutely: 'Before Generation X even had a name, John Hughes gave it a voice' (Rottenberg 2009: 28).

The specific story of *The Breakfast Club* was one that struck a chord with contemporary audiences because of this focus on a youth perspective. One of the primary ways it was able to do so was by focusing the narrative on the five main teen characters. By telling their story, the film calls attention to the trials and tribulations of youth but also made significant inroads into how the teen genre itself is perceived. The film makes explicit, and thereby crystalizes, the elements that audiences have come to expect from the teen genre: the iconic character types, the breaking down of stereotypes to reveal individual personalities, the primacy of the peer group, the power of internal pressure, the conflict between generations, the budding romances, the importance of the high school setting, and the focus on achieving self-acceptance and self-actualization.

The Breakfast Club was able to address all these genre concerns, to clearly manifest these paradigmatic teen film tropes, while also offering trenchant commentary on issues of contemporary relevance to teens and to the population at large. While anxieties over the double standards between genders and concerns about income gaps and class disparities are important to many teens trying to navigate their way through the microcosm of high school, these matters were of prominent relevance in the largely conservative and materialistic Reagan-era 1980s. During the decade, disputes were raging over women's rights and conflicts were brewing about how best to address the unequal distribution of wealth. Essentially, wars were being fought on domestic fronts, and the film did not shy away from these clashes.

While *The Breakfast Club* is not without its problems, including troubling gender politics, underdeveloped depictions of adults, and contrived couplings, it nonetheless still endures as an archetypal teen film. Analyzing its component parts and the context in which it was made sheds light on the teen film genre as a whole, on the 1980s, and helps explain why the film is still so meaningful.

Situating *The Breakfast Club* within a brief history of the teen film

The history of both the word 'teenager' and of the teen film genre itself is intricate, involving a number of social, economic, political, and cultural forces. Often, the concept of the teenager is traced back to 1904 when

G. Stanley Hall coined the term 'adolescent' to note a distinct period of development between childhood and adulthood (Hall 1904). Previously, this liminal stage, while it existed biologically and in preparation for demarcated rites of passage such as religious ceremonies, was not a separate time of life: children often went to work at young ages, educational opportunities were limited, and leisure time, especially for the working classes, was minimal. It was not until the 1920s that the term 'teenage' was used to describe a boy or girl and not until the 1950s that term 'teenager' entered more common usage (Barnhart and Metcalf 1997: 234). Not coincidentally, these were two decades noted for their economic prosperity, when teens started to be seen as a distinct cohort, and with that, as a demographic group that advertisers could target. One of the ways this marketing trend became manifest was by making films featuring teenagers.

Technically, there have always been people in their teens on film, that is, characters between the ages of 13 and 19 who appear on screen. There is a long and rich history of teens on film and the teen film genre that has been previously detailed in works by Considine (1985), Doherty (2002), Shary (2002), Driscoll (2011), and Nelson (2011). Instead of tracing the complete corpus of films with teen characters and the teen film genre, however, the focus in this book primarily draws on dramatic films, with an emphasis on the thematic topics of juvenile delinquency and on the causes for rebelliousness, because of their more direct influence on *The Breakfast Club*.

A common conception is that the teen film began in the 1950s, the only decade prior to the 1980s when there was such a large and sustained production trend of films featuring teenage characters. Arguably, though, while the genre may have started to take more distinct shape in the 1950s, the teen film can be seen to have its beginnings in the 1920s when teenagers started to become a market force (Felando 2000: 86) and when teenage characters had important roles in dramatic films more broadly defined. Films such as *The Road to Ruin* (Parker 1928) depicts the downfall of a teen girl because of sex and drugs, and the film series featuring the Dead End Kids (primarily between 1937–39) dealt with adolescents coping with the downturned economy during the years of the Great Depression. Importantly, while these were characters in various sorts of trouble, the source of the problems was seen as coming from societal forces, and the hope was that by addressing these large-scale issues, the problems could be resolved.

While young adult women were pivotal characters in films like *Stella Dallas* (Vidor 1937) and *Mildred Pierce* (Curtiz 1945), two films where mothers martyr themselves for their daughters, the films cannot be said to be teen films because the narrative focus is primarily on the parents (as the titles indicate). However, the importance of the young characters is evident because so many plot points hinge upon them. The films still ostensibly frame the problematic situation as socially based because of the women's drive toward upward financial mobility, while also planting the seeds for illustrating how underlying crises, resulting from gender strife and (in *Mildred Pierce*'s case) post-war consumer culture, were germinating in shifting family dynamics. Significantly, at the time, the resolution of the conflicts ultimately lay in the hands of the parents.

The 1950s marked a near tectonic shift in the representation of teens on film. The historical context of the decade is significant: economic prosperity led to teens having disposable income and to them being courted as a distinct market segment; the move to the suburbs was met with addressing women's changing social and familial roles, especially after so many found work outside the home during World War II; and in terms of the film industry, the *Paramount* case, which forced studios to divest themselves of the their theater chains and therefore their guaranteed exhibition outlets, the move away from cities and out of proximity to the most profitable first-run theaters, and the rise of the competing new medium of television, all made Hollywood rethink its strategies in order to stem audience attrition. As Thomas Doherty argues in *Teenagers and Teenpics*, one of the tactics used was to appeal to teenagers, who were emerging as the most reliable movie-going demographic segment (2002: 188).

The appeals to teens were evident in exploitation films of the era targeted directly toward the cohort, seen especially with films from American International Pictures (AIP) like *I Was a Teenage Werewolf* (Fowler Jr. 1957), *Reform School Girl* (Bernds 1957), and *High School Hellcats* (Bernds 1958). AIP's 'Peter Pan' marketing strategy essentially boiled down to making films that appealed to older teenage boys in order to attract the largest possible audience; the logic was that girls and younger boys would all go to see what nineteen-year-old males liked (Doherty 2002: 128). However, the two most influential films of the decade were mainstream Hollywood fare. *Rebel Without a Cause* (Ray 1955) and *Blackboard Jungle* (Brooks 1955), released in the same year, were two social problem films about juvenile delinquency. *Rebel*, which showed redeemable teenagers who were *in* trouble, and *Blackboard*, which showed irredeemable teenagers who *were* trouble, presented two sides to the growing fears around teen rebellion and the sense of discontent with the status quo of American values.

Again, it is important to consider from where the problems stem and where the solutions originate; both films present overdetermined narratives in these regards. The breakdown of traditional family and gender roles indicates the parents are to blame in *Rebel*, while the criminal behavior of the teens in *Blackboard* results from entire government, social, and educational systems that have failed. Reconciliation and reintegration, if possible, occur because the adults reassert their authority. However, the narrative leap the films make is significant: they both substantiate a new point of view that the problems lay with adults and authority and that the teens' voices in protest of these shortcomings are valid.

These strains of substantiated protest became even more pronounced in the 1960s and 1970s. While 'clean teen' (Doherty 2002: 153) films were still released, such as the lighthearted Beach Blanket Bingo series, teen film production in general saw a downturn as a dramatic art cinema with somewhat older youth in primary roles became popular. Called a 'Hollywood renaissance' (Schatz 1993: 20) because of the influence of modernism and the European New Waves, films like *The Graduate* (Nichols 1967) and *Easy Rider* (Hopper 1969) featured youth rebelling against the establishment more generally, especially in the wake of Vietnam and economic crises. While the general shape of American society was evidently to blame, the solutions were practically nonexistent and authority and tradition were the enemy.

Meanwhile, teen films were still produced during the 1970s, but they took on a different bent. Brickman argues in *New American Teenagers* that because of the political and financial crises decentering power, civil rights movements giving voice to women and minorities, and the 'Me' generation focusing on individual self-help, a unified national identity was giving way and allowing diverse 'others' to assert their individuality (2012: 18). As a result, instead of the predominantly white, heterosexual, middle-class male that was often at the center of teen narratives (and studies of teen films), the rise of identity politics led to the production of teen films with more marginalized groups at the center. Youth-oriented films like *Badlands* (Malick 1973), *Ode to Billy Joe* (Baer 1976), and *Rock 'n' Roll High School* (Arkush 1979) told stories about girls, homosexuality, and misfits (respectively). Rather than being reconciled into the dominant culture, the teens move away from it (ibid.: 24), illustrating continued problems with traditional patriarchal authority, which was no longer perceived to be in control.

As the Hollywood Renaissance and the counterculture started to recede in the later 1970s, and as large-scale blockbusters were becoming popular, some more mainstream teen films were again being released, priming the way for the resurgence of the trend in the 1980s. While the closest lineage to the teen angst of *The Breakfast Club* are films of the social problem, juvenile delinquent, and youth rebellion ilk, other types are also influential. Horror films like *Texas Chainsaw Massacre* (Hooper 1974) and *Halloween* (Carpenter 1978) deal with punishing female sexuality and show the resilience of the final girl (Clover 1992) to overcome and survive the threat mostly on her own; few authority figures are to be seen or trusted. *Grease* (Kleiser 1978) depicts a variety of social groups in high school and the difficulties inherent in crossing the boundaries between them, along with making the somewhat rebellious 'greasers' cooler than the 'clean teens.' Meanwhile, *Over the Edge* (Kaplan 1979) deals with kids in the suburbs who are so full of anger and boredom, especially after their parents threaten to take away the one place in the community where they are allowed to congregate, that they decide to burn down their school. This film in particular approaches teen delinquency with complexity, suggesting that the problems and solutions are multifaceted. As Jay Scott (1983: 64) points out in his review of the film, 'the solution is as protean as the problem'; it is the parents and the schools, societal and economic issues, troubled kids and injustice that are all cause for concern, and there is no easy fix.

The variety of teen films in the latter part of the '70s foretells the array of genre entries that would appear in the following decade. In addition, the box-office success of these films, along with that of the youth-targeted blockbusters in the 1970s, the competition arising from new home entertainment options like cable and home video, and, according to Shary in *Generation Multiplex* (2002: 6), the burgeoning multiplex cinemas springing up in shopping malls, all led to the increase in production of teen films in the 1980s. The demographic was again being enticed with films that featured teen characters, this time in an even wider variety with updated stories to appeal to contemporary youth, ranging from teen comedies, dramas, and romances to action-adventure and horror films (and even science fiction and westerns, like *Back to the Future* (Zemeckis 1985) and *Young Guns* (Cain 1988), respectively). Indeed, while it is useful to situate *The Breakfast Club* in the historical trajectory of teen rebel films, it is also important to note its contemporary context: the film appeared during the surging production trend of teen films, and films of the genre took on a range of subject matter and were of various tones.

In the 1980s, there was more variety even within the frame of the teen rebel films. *Ferris Bueller's Day Off* (1986) depicts in comedic form students cutting school for a day, and its title character is filled with *joie de vivre*, while *Risky Business* (Brickman 1983) is a twisted take on how to succeed in life and business through lawbreaking with prostitutes and brothels. The action-war films *Red Dawn* (Milius 1986) and *Iron Eagle* (Furie 1986) show teens defying government and military orders to save themselves and their parents' lives. Meanwhile *Footloose* (Ross 1984) and *Dirty Dancing* (Ardolino 1987) both show rebellion through forbidden dancing and censured romance. Even the teen suicide storyline had a range: *Dead Poets Society* (Weir 1989) features a teen who rebels against his father's wishes and then kills himself instead of suffering through his punishment, and *Heathers* (Lehmann 1989), replete with a character literally named 'J.D.' (Juvenile delinquent), presents a satire of teen life and its social constructs. The decade also saw teens on the border and on the flip side of the juvenile delinquent coin – there are the kids who are in trouble, for whom there is hope and justification outside themselves for their actions, versus those who are trouble and who are irredeemable. Bender in *The Breakfast Club* straddles the distinction, while a variety of rebel types populate films like *My Bodyguard* (Bill 1980), *The Outsiders* (Coppola 1983), and *Stand by Me* (Reiner 1986).

The scope of the films, both the larger genre and the specific teen rebellion stories, illustrates how the teen film was maturing during the decade. Over this development process, the films could themselves be further broken down into subgenres, for example, the high school film, teen romance, teen rebellion, etc., or alternatively, survival/protection, love/sex, angst/rebellion, ambition/dreams, celebration/leisure (Nelson 2011: 424–425), and were also often categorized as hybrids with other genres (e.g., *Friday the 13th* (Cunningham 1980) is teen and horror; *Grease 2* (Birch 1982) is teen, musical, and romantic comedy; *The Goonies* (Donner 1985) is teen and action-adventure). Indeed, one of the reasons for considering *The Breakfast Club* an archetype of the form is twofold. It neatly encompasses distinctive teen film genre elements, such as iconic teen character types and generational conflict in a school setting. In addition, it clearly fits within the boundaries of the teen film without the mapping and mixing of other elements from other content-based genres, such as action or science fiction (versus genres of tone like comedy or drama).

The Breakfast Club, as well as other teen films from the 1980s, also develops the rebellion narrative in marked difference from previous decades. In part, films of the time were able to tackle issues on a more 'adult' level because of both the new ratings system that included a 'PG-13' category, which allowed for more risqué content, and because ratings were easy to get around, either at the movie theater or via home entertainment options. As more than just a factor of ratings, though, to a greater extent than prior films in earlier decades, the teens are the primary focus of the narrative. Authority figures, although they significantly influence the teens' lives, are mostly absent. Effectively, as generational conflict foments because of parents' and authorities' absence, incompetence, or corruption, the teens form communities unto themselves.

As a result of the teens existing in their own distinct social groupings, the teen films of the 1980s generally, and *The Breakfast Club* specifically, aim to address teens more directly, take teen problems seriously, and appear to be told from a teen perspective. Consequently, the narratively framed sources of the problems and the solutions for teen angst and rebellion change as well. In the 1930s and 1940s, society and the environment were to blame, and authority had to take charge; in the 1950s, it was the changing family structure, and parents had to reassert their power; in the 1960s and 1970s, it was the establishment as a whole, and there was little hope all around. In the 1980s, the factors combined and were multiple; teens were affected by failing institutions and the shortcomings of authority figures, as well as by internal and external pressure and by boredom and disillusionment. What was abundantly clear, however, was where the solutions lay: teens had to gain knowledge and figure out problems on their own.

Structuring the study of *The Breakfast Club*

Arguing that *The Breakfast Club* represents the quintessential teen film among all the varieties of films in the genre is a bold statement. Importantly, however, this is not to say that *The Breakfast Club* is a perfect film, nor is it saying that it is exemplary and by doing so, to commit the crime of synecdoche, to say that this one film can stand in for all teen films. However, because it does offer such a representative, crystalized model of the form, and because it of its continued commercial success, it stands out as an archetypal teen film. As such, analyzing both its textual and contextual components can shed light on the teen film genre as a whole and on why this film in particular endures.

Looking to genre theory supports the claim of *The Breakfast Club* as an exemplar. On a general foundational level, the teen film can be defined as featuring characters in prominent roles who are between the ages of 13 and 19 (allowing the main, but not sole, focus to be on the high school years), and the film fits squarely in this demarcation. However, while often there is one primary feature that is used to define a genre – in this case, the age of the characters – there are almost always other descriptors and levels of meaning attached that solidify this status. For example, labeling something a western signifies more than just a film that takes place 'out west'; further qualifications are needed to denote genre, whether regarding the content of the films, their tone/affect, or their context of production and consumption. As such, saying teen films are about teen characters is a necessary but not sufficient qualification to determine the status of the films as a genre.

Generally, in order to form a coherent or cohesive genre on a textual level, there is a strong tie between what Rick Altman would call the films' semantic and syntactic dimensions, where the semantic refers to the building blocks of the text, like the iconography, setting, and character types, and the syntactic relates to the ways these building blocks are organized, for example in the plot structure or in the relationships between the characters (Altman 2012 (1984): 31). While the distinctions between what is considered 'semantic' and what is considered 'syntactic' are debated, the conceptual framework is still highly instructive. As audiences, we have come to expect certain repeated elements in the teen film, and while not every genre film will have every element, what is notable about *The Breakfast Club* is how many generic elements it exemplifies so explicitly, including iconic tropes of setting, character types, and thematics.

Additionally, besides textually, Altman notes in *Film/Genre* (1999: 14) that there are three other levels upon which genres can be understood: production, marketing, and reception. For example, certain studios can produce, or filmmakers and creative personnel can often work in, a particular genre, and thus their very association or presence can suggest a genre classification. Readily identifiable and repeated elements used in marketing and promotion strategies, such as designs of one-sheets, formats of trailers, publicity, and merchandizing, signal likelihood of film type. And reception, including the discourse of critic responses and audience expectations, also frame understandings of genre. Taken together, these areas are further sites outside the text that enunciate film categorization.

The significance and understanding of labels lie not just in how the films are classified though. A basic way to think of genre is to look at Barry Keith Grant's statement that 'genre movies are those commercial feature films which, through repetition and variation, tell familiar stories with familiar characters in familiar situations' (2003: xv). But on a more complex level, genre films serve other ritual and ideological functions as well. As cultural products, films are sites for the articulation of ideology; furthermore, as Thomas Schatz explains in *Hollywood Genres* (1981: 263), genres function like myths in that they are ways of addressing and momentarily resolving larger social conflicts and cultural contradictions that often cannot be so neatly resolved in reality. Using the structuralist intervention, and applying it to the study of genre and genre films, shows how the central underlying issues remain over time, but that specific films are contemporary embodiments of those long-standing concerns. By expressing the values of the time and place in which they are produced, films of a genre tackle enduring cultural problems.

As Will Wright explains in *Six Guns and Society*, a study that examines the western genre within a structuralist frame, 'the structure of myth is assumed to be universal; it can be derived from an analysis of any instance of myth and the requirements of symbolic communication. But the formal structure of myth is embodied in a symbolic content that is socially specific' (1975: 11). The teen film, then, specifically of the 1980s and *The Breakfast Club* in particular, can be understood to focus on universal cultural problems central to the genre: How do teens navigate the coming-of-age process and become self-actualized? How do they find their place in the world, one that has been damaged by the previous generation, while retaining a sense of themselves and being true to their values? Although conflict with authority is a main concern of the teen film and of the teen rebel specifically, it is important to note that it is only one (albeit highly illustrative and often repeated) way through which this identity formation process progresses. The teen film addresses the coming-of-age transformation on many levels: the central conflicts are external between youth and authority and between different members of the peer group, and internal as the teens discover a confident sense of self. Also, as with most genre films, the narrative-based resolutions to the conflicts are merely temporary solutions to the larger problems teens face in their everyday worlds.

The Breakfast Club embodies all these attributes, clearly articulating and clarifying the elements of the teen film genre. Looking at the multiple ways teen films are defined and enunciated, what they represent, and how an exemplary film can highlight these ideals, this book approaches an analysis of *The Breakfast Club* by examining its content in terms of narrative, theme, and characters, as well as its context of production, marketing, and reception. Because of the importance of the teen market in the 1980s, the first chapter will begin with an analysis of the state of the Hollywood industry during the decade, illustrating how the market was primed for the onslaught of teen films and how *The Breakfast Club* was able to capitalize on the burgeoning success of the genre. In addition, the specific ways the film was able to appeal to the youth market had as much to do with the changing marketplace as with the actors available for the roles. The chapter will also address how the talent and cast came together as the result of opportune circumstances.

Specific content elements are the subject of the next two chapters. The centrality of the cast and the roles each inhabited cannot be overstated in terms of their importance to creating such an exemplary film. As such, Chapter 2 will go into an in-depth discussion of the iconic character types on display. The characters are significant not just because they are seen as representative teen film archetypes but also because of the peeling away of the layers behind these narrative constructions. By first building up and then breaking down the stereotypes, *The Breakfast Club* is able to both construct and deconstruct teen film tropes at the same time.

Essential to the story and to its time of production in the 1980s are the political, economic, and social issues the country was facing. Chapter 3 takes a cultural studies approach to examine how contemporary concerns dealing with gender, sexuality, and class are addressed in the film, and what it means that certain subjects are ignored, such as diversity and larger political matters. Additionally, this chapter will focus on generational conflict. Generation X was the generation coming of age during the decade, and even though it had yet to be given a label, there were already associations of this cohort with qualities of cynicism and disillusionment. Baby boomers, the supposedly idealist generation that came of age in the decades prior, meanwhile, were still seen as trying to hold on to youthful attributes and, in the process, were shirking adult responsibilities. Conflicts arose as members of Generation X felt like they had to take on mature roles even though they did not have role models to guide them. *The Breakfast Club* illustrates the complex effects of the oppositions between youth and adults.

The emphasis on character types and the attention placed on generational conflict in the film itself carried over into the way the film was distributed and marketed. Posters and trailers for *The Breakfast Club* clearly draw attention to the different character types to try to appeal to a range of teen audiences. At the same time, the film's 'R' rating conveyed its adult sensibilities and mature storylines, in effect broadening its appeal to older audiences. In combination with the top-selling soundtrack and videos in rotation on MTV, the marketing for the film contributed to the way *The Breakfast Club* was positioned in the corpus of the teen genre and is the context of production focus of Chapter 4.

While the marketing clearly positioned its youth market appeal, the immediate response to the film also bolstered its label as a quality film that could speak to multiple audiences. *The Breakfast Club* is one of the few teen films that enjoyed box-office and (albeit mixed) critical success upon its release, has attained a 'cult' following, and continues to be lauded, as well as picked apart, in the press. Many of the critical assessments of the film also bring up the importance of the singular talent of John Hughes and his influence on the voice of the teen characters created. Chapter 5 will examine how the critical and popular reception of the film and its director cemented their place in the teen film canon. Additionally, this concluding chapter will look at the impact *The Breakfast Club* continues to have on popular culture. The film is repeatedly referenced either directly or in homages in later teen films, is often the subject of 1980s and teen film retrospectives, and new releases of the DVD and re-releases of the film in theaters occur at regular intervals. The impact and legacy of *The Breakfast Club* persists even more than 30 years after its initial release, serving as a testament to the film's lasting relevance.

While it can be hard to pinpoint, a succinct description of the teen film is that it is about teens gaining confidence in themselves as they mature; a useful and more specific working definition of the teen film genre is that it

> is marked by teens who go through a coming-of-age process in which they question who they are and who they want to be, both as individuals and as part of a group. This process of becoming self-actualized occurs as they find an identity distinct from the previous generation, celebrate and survive adolescence, and recognize the significance of their current actions.
> (Nelson 2017: 128)

Naturally, the description of a genre should also be applicable to specific genre films, and indeed, *The Breakfast Club* fits this classification. The five teens discover who they are as individuals, learn who the others in the group are, and figure out their place in the larger social groupings of the high school. They do so while braving conflicts with adults, taking time to celebrate youth, and realizing how important the decisions they make and the actions they take in the present are to their future.

More than just embodying these elements of the teen film as genre, what Hughes did with *The Breakfast Club* was help introduce, blend, and propagate multiple generic features that would come to be expected with the teen film formula. The structure of the film, including iconic character types, settings, conflicts, and maturation and development processes, are all displayed and articulated throughout. This content, combined with its context of production in the middle of a boom in teen filmmaking, and the marketing, which focused on contemporary music, peer group dynamics, and generational conflict, merged with an enthusiastic reception by youth audiences. Everything coalesced to solidify the status of *The Breakfast Club* as one of the most emblematic films of the 1980s and one of the most definitive teen films of the genre.

1 The right place at the right time

How the market was primed for the production of *The Breakfast Club*

In the 1980s, economic factors within the Hollywood industry and economic factors in the United States at large helped ready the market for the huge onslaught of teen film productions. Teen films, which came to be recognized as those films featuring primarily teenage characters going through coming-of-age processes, appeared in multiple forms. They could be seen as subgenres of, or hybrids with, larger, more established genres, such as teen comedies or teen horrors, or they could be divided into specific types of the larger umbrella category of the teen film, such as teen love/sex films or teen angst/rebellion films (Nelson 2011: 423). Regardless of their specific classification, they were plentiful. From 1980 to 1989, over 460 teen films were released, accounting for a little more than 10% of all films released in the United States (Shary 2002; Nelson 2011: 168).

Not only were teen films being produced in large numbers, but they were also some of the more successful films released as well, as determined by box-office success. From 1980 to 1989, teen films made up approximately one of every ten films released but about one of every six of the top box-office films of the year, or about 16%. In 1985, the year *The Breakfast Club* was released, teen films made up almost 12% of all films released but a whopping 24% of the top 50 grossing films of the year (Nelson 2011: 169). In addition, because they often had smaller production budgets than the large-scale blockbusters or studio pictures with big-name stars and their commensurate big-name salaries, the ROI, or return on investment, for teen films was greater as well. As a case in point, the budget for *The Breakfast Club* was reported in *Variety* as being in the $6 to $9 million range (Tusher 1985), while the worldwide box office was reported at $51.5 million according to *Box Office Mojo* (2018); these numbers do not even take into account money made from ancillary markets, such as cable and home video. In general, teen films were less risky and came with the potential for great reward.

Hollywood may have appeared to be doing well as a result of blockbuster filmmaking and increasing total box-office receipts; further analysis into the numbers and into what was going on behind the scenes, however, reveals a different picture. Studio fears of box-office attrition during the decade were founded. While total box office increased from $2.75 billion in 1980 to $5.02 billion in 1990, the actual number of tickets sold held relatively steady from 1.02 to 1.06 billion over the decade, meaning that the increases were due largely to rising ticket prices, which averaged $2.69 in 1980 and $4.75 in 1990 (MPA 1990 US Economic Review). These numbers also do not take into account the soaring negative costs and mounting costs of prints and advertising, which, while not including increasing returns from ancillary markets, outpaced domestic box-office revenues (ibid.). Hollywood needed to figure out ways to lure audiences back into theaters, and making teen films, of which *The Breakfast Club* turned out to be exemplary, was one of the key strategies.

The rest of this chapter examines the changing nature of the film and media business in the 1980s, including how competing home entertainment technologies affected audiences and how changing ownership structures and modes of production affected Hollywood output. Because the focus is both on the teen film more broadly and *The Breakfast Club* more specifically, the first part of these analyses will look at industrial factors affecting the industry and economic elements that can help situate the film. The second part will go into detail about the production history of *The Breakfast Club* and how the specific cast and crew that was available, including the young talent and the more experienced filmmakers, assembled at a particular moment in Hollywood history. *The Breakfast Club* would not have existed, nor would it have had its lasting effect, if the market had not been primed and if the creative personnel were not in the right place at the right time.

The changing Hollywood industry and its effect on teen film production

There are many similarities between Hollywood in the 1980s and in the 1950s. Both periods saw a booming economy (for certain socioeconomic classes), competition from new technologies, and government policies that affected the film industry. Not coincidentally, the two decades are also the most prolific in terms of teen film production and remain the two decades that are most closely associated with teen films, which can in large part be ascribed to these economic conditions (Nelson 2017: 126).

The 1950s and the mid-1980s are both considered periods of economic growth because of markers such as increased gross domestic product and low unemployment rates ('United States' 2007: 1020–1021). Although not all sectors of the population were beneficiaries of these booms, neverthe-less, teenagers, often the ones from middle-class families, were viewed as reaping some of the rewards. Teenagers, whose families were prospering in the 1950s, and who had more money as a result of living in two-income families where both parents worked and because they themselves had jobs in the 1980s, were seen as having the coveted 'disposable income.' Because they usually did not have to pay household expenses, the money they had could be spent on non-necessities, such as entertainment purchases. As their buying power increased, producers and advertisers paid them more attention, and they became a bona fide market segment. Some estimates from research companies in the 1980s put teen discretionary income buying power at over $30 billion per year (van Tuyl 1989: 14). Trying to figure out what they liked became a big business as research firms were enlisted to study their habits and desires and goods were catered to their tastes.

Indeed, this focus on marketing across businesses was exceedingly important for Hollywood in the 1980s. The amount of money spent on marketing, which happens in multiple stages of production (for example, when assessing audience tastes and testing films before release and when advertising films once they have already been made), grew exponentially during the decade. However, it actually became a prominent tendency in the film business starting in the 1950s, and the reason for this increased emphasis on marketing reveals some of the ways Hollywood views its products and audiences. In the years following the Paramount Consent Decrees in 1948, the vertically integrated major studios lost their guaranteed exhibition outlets, meaning that instead of making films that would be released in theaters regardless of quality, studios that were now focused primarily on production and distribution had to be more concerned with actually selling their products to exhibitors and audiences. In addition, with the rise of television as a competing entertainment technology for audience attention, viewers became more discerning about which movies they would go out to see in the theater.

Industry structure also played a role in the increased focus on marketing starting toward the end of the studio system. Picking up momentum in the 1960s during the first wave of mergers and acquisitions that swept through Hollywood, studios were bought by larger corporations, companies that were more familiar with marketing research techniques from their experience in packaged goods (Wyatt 1994: 156). Marketing research would help the studios' film production decisions look financially sound to their corporate owners. The next big wave of mergers and acquisitions began in the 1980s when studios were bought by large conglomerates that also had other media holdings, and the need to focus on marketing increased. Combined with the shift in distribution strategies in the 1970s that often followed wide, saturation release patterns, where films would be released on hundreds and then thousands of screens around the country simultaneously, and with the commensurate television advertising campaigns that would ensure the big advertising push needed to make audiences aware of new releases, marketing became essential. As Mark Litwak describes when talking about the state of the industry in the 1980s, 'executives increasingly make decisions based on market research, demographic trends and minimizing financial risks' (1986: 97).

With the increasing focus of marketing in general duly noted, the importance of targeting teens specifically was of huge concern during the decade. Not only did they have a large amount of disposable income as youth research reports revealed, but commissioned research reports also revealed that over 80% of the youth population went to the movies ('Youth Barometer' 1985: 2). Teens also made up a large portion of the movie-going audience, and even more important, they were frequent moviegoers, often going to the theater multiple times per month, and were repeat viewers, who would go to see the same film again and again (Albert 1985). In mid-decade, according to an 'Incidence of Motion Picture Attendance' report cited in *Variety* by Jack Valenti, the long-time head of the MPAA, the youth audience, or those in the age bracket between twelve and twenty years old, made up 36% of total yearly admissions in 1984, even though they only made up 18% of the resident civilian population (Valenti 1985: 94). In other words, even though teens made up less than a fifth of the population, they made up more than a third of those who went to the movies. In addition, the same report revealed that frequent moviegoers made up 84% of theater admissions, and the teenage segment of twelve- to seventeen-year-olds made up 45% of those frequent moviegoers (ibid.). Because films featuring teenaged characters were thought to appeal to this desired demographic, Hollywood started producing more teen films.

Another reason for the increase in teen film production is because Hollywood tends to follow patterns; when it notices downturns in the box office, it falls back on familiar strategies that were successful in the past. So when there are threats of audience attrition because of competing media, the tendency was for there to be a subsequent increase in the production of teen films. In the 1950s, television threatened the box office with Hollywood thinking that it would have to fight and curtail the television beast in order to retain studio revenues. Eventually, Hollywood learned how to profit from television, largely by getting into production of television programming and later, especially in the eras of media deregulation in the 1980s and 1990s, by having ownership stakes in television networks (Anderson 1994; Hilmes 2014). Combined with the migrations to the suburbs and away from expensive first-run theaters, a greater portion of the population was opting to stay home to be entertained instead of going out to the movies. The hope was that teen films would entice the teen audience to go to the movies in order to socialize with their peers.

In the 1980s, competing media again seemed to be a threat. While cable and home videocassettes were introduced in the 1970s, their popularity increased dramatically in the 1980s (Wasser 2001; Mullen 2003). Indeed, the diffusion of innovation was rapid: in 1980, of all households that had televisions, 2.4% had VCRs; in 1989, the penetration rate was 70.2% (MPAA 2000 Economic Review). Again, Hollywood initially fought the new technologies because of fears that audiences would rather stay home to watch films on television instead of in the theater (Wasko 1994: 114). And indeed, audiences did turn to these new technologies; by 1987, the home entertainment market was more profitable for studios than the theatrical box office (Thompson and Bordwell 2010: 663). However, as with television, Hollywood profited by offering sales and rentals of their films on videocassette, by licensing rights to cable stations and later in having partnerships in stations either outright or through studios' conglomerate owners, and by producing films for direct release onto cable and home video. Savvy to the changing market, Hollywood again turned to teen films. Even though reports in *Variety* noted that teens, although still a large part of the theatrical audience, reduced their theatrical attendance by 20% in 1985, they tripled their rate of viewing rentals on VHS the same year (Roth 1986: 3). To get teens both to the theaters and interested in rentals for new 'VCR dates,' they had to make products that appealed to the market segment.

Another trend influencing the prolific production of teen films is Hollywood's tendency to follow cyclical production and marketing patterns after a few similar popular releases. As Eleanor Bergstein, the writer and co-producer of *Dirty Dancing* (1987), stated, 'Never underestimate Hollywood's eagerness to copy something successful' (quoted in Freeman 2016: 157). Copying recent successes showed itself in a few ways. First, just as in the 1950s when the success of *Rebel Without a Cause* and *Blackboard Jungle*, both in 1955, influenced the teen production trend later in the decade, there were a few teen films that were surprise box-office hits in the late 1970s and early 1980s that spurred the filmmaking trend into the latter decade. Films like *Halloween* and *Breaking Away* (Yates) both in 1978, as well as the successes of *Friday the 13th* (1980) and *Porky's* (Clark 1982), led the studios to produce similar films, thinking this was the genre teens wanted to see. Even though cycles of popularity tend to run their course, it was still worth it to ride the wave for as long as it would last.

Other ways Hollywood copied recent successes and applied them to teen filmmaking and marketing in the 1980s could be seen in its turns toward the strategies of making easily accessible films with broad appeal. Blockbuster filmmaking began in earnest in the 1970s with *Jaws* (Spielberg 1975) and *Star Wars* (Lucas 1977), where Hollywood deliberately tried to target teens with easy-to-follow, action-oriented plots and with summer releases that appealed to students on their summer vacations. This was combined with the rise of the multiplex in malls across the country, where the increasing number of movie screens in shopping centers frequented by teens led to a need for more youth-targeted films (Shary 2002: 6). Making films accessible meant making them easy to understand, fun to watch, and ensuring there were ample ways, places, and times to see them.

Around the same time, two other buzz terms for Hollywood strategies that also tried to benefit from widespread audience tastes generally and the teen market specifically were gaining a foothold: 'high concept' and 'synergy.' Justin Wyatt describes high concept as a production style based on ' "the look, the hook, and the book." The look of the images, the marketing hooks, and the reduced narratives form the cornerstones of high concept' (Wyatt 1994: 22). High production values, sleek designs, and streamlined plots were cornerstones of this strategy, providing popular and easily palatable entertainment for the masses who watched movies, of which teens were a primary percentage. Synergy, meanwhile, is the idea that products related to one intellectual property, if sold across different media and ancillary markets, could exponentially increase sales and recognition of said property. In 1980s filmmaking, this meant that the box office of a film could be enhanced if there were also a successful soundtrack accompanying it. This was a mutually beneficial practice – the sales of both the film and the soundtrack would be bolstered by sales and publicity of the product across markets.

The proliferation of entertainment media in multiple markets that could be exploited using the practice of synergy also meant that there was a need for product, especially product that would appeal to the demographic that spent so much of its money on entertainment purchases. Multiplexes, video store shelves, and cable stations all needed content. As Thomas Schatz (1993: 35) describes, there were three dominant modes of production in the New Hollywood, or the period beginning post-*Jaws*: blockbusters, star vehicles, and small, independent films. But it is important to add another mode – the genre picture. Budget-wise, some of these genre pictures were mid-budget films made by the major studios. During the 1980s, teen films of all different types and from different sectors of the industry were produced.

Using the teen films *Flashdance* (Lyne) and *Footloose*, released one year apart from each other in 1983 and 1984, respectively, illustrates how these filmmaking strategies were applied with great success to teen films. Both *Flashdance* and *Footloose* were distributed by Paramount, had easy-to-follow plots and glossy production designs, and were in the top ten box-office hits of the year. They both had the number one top-selling soundtrack albums of their years of release ('The '80s Soundtracks' 1989), which was partly achieved by pushing their related music videos on the nascent MTV cable channel. In another indication of the burgeoning symbiotic relationship between the new media technologies, the box office for both titles increased when each was released on videocassette while the films were still in theaters (Bierbaum 1984: 3), indicating the benefits of cross-promotion and synergy across ancillary markets.

It was in this media industry environment that the teen film was flourishing in the 1980s. While the recognition of the importance of the teenage market could not be ignored, the essential question remained, however, of what specifically would appeal to this audience. An appropriately titled article in *Variety*, 'Youth May Be Wasted on Young but Its Appeal Is Showbiz Asset If You Understand What It Is' (Albert 1985: 7), demonstrates this point and states that Hollywood was trying to cater to the market with youth-targeted products. This often manifested in the form of entertainment featuring teen performers.

But it was not enough just to have films starring teenaged characters. The article quoted research studies commissioned at the time that tried to focus on what youth wanted to see more specifically. The report revealed that the demographic preferred films with cross-generational appeal instead of feeling like they were being pandered to, and that unlike adults, youth audiences will go out to the movies to be shocked. Interestingly, the reports also concluded that youth would rather 'see a film that is passionately involving' rather than necessarily sexual, and that they want to feel as though they have had an involving or passionate experience that they would like to go through themselves 'without having to undergo any of the dangers' (ibid.). Marketing research during the 1980s set the stage for many different types of films that could satisfy these requirements and the wide range of teenage tastes.

While qualifications about teens wanting to have emotional experiences at the movies seem to describe *The Breakfast Club* accurately, the studios preferred comedies like *Porky's* and horrors like *Friday the 13th* that had already proved their strong track records. They were, however, willing to take chances on teen films of different stripes, including dramas and romances. And so teen films of various types and with a range of budgets were in production throughout the 1980s because of the importance of the teen audience and the potential for solid investment returns. But even with all the marketing and carefully planned strategies, there was no guarantee that a film would be profitable, that it would get the support it needed from its studio, or that it would resonate with audiences. Sometimes, a confluence of circumstances, timing, and just the right personnel is necessary for making a film a success.

Behind the scenes and in front of the camera: the production of *The Breakfast Club*

The most widely recognizable names and faces of *The Breakfast Club* are its director John Hughes and its primary cast of young actors: Molly Ringwald, Anthony Michael Hall, Emilio Estevez, Ally Sheedy, and Judd Nelson. While these names are the most famous and familiar, there are a number of additional people, in the cast and crew but also studio personnel, who all contributed to making the film the touchstone it remains. What follows is a production history of how the film came together, but instead of a completely linear story, this part of the chapter examines some of the individuals, groups of people, and companies involved behind the scenes and the important roles they undertook. Later chapters will also go into further detail about some of the players as their contributions relate to areas such as the marketing and reception of the film.

The director: John Hughes

John Hughes was one of the most successful filmmakers of the 1980s and into the early 1990s. The *New York Times* reported in 1991, after the release of *Home Alone* (Columbus) in 1990, which he wrote but did not direct, that he had a striking run of nineteen scripts made into movies starting in 1982, and almost all of them were profitable (Carter 1991). Because of his ability to crank out box-office draws and because his teen films especially, such as *Sixteen Candles*, *Ferris Bueller's Day Off*, and *Pretty in Pink*, struck such a cord with audiences, he was labeled a 'philosopher of youth' by Roger Ebert (1986) and dubbed both a 'teen laureate' and 'sweet bard of youth' in *Vanity Fair* after his untimely death from a heart attack in 2009 (Kamp 2010b).

Both because of his renown as a filmmaker and his close association with 1980s teen films, much has been written about his history, including full-length books, such as Susannah Gora's *You Couldn't Ignore Me If You Tried: The Brat Pack, John Hughes, and Their Impact on a Generation* (2010), Thomas Christie's *John Hughes and Eighties Cinema: Teenage Hopes and American Dreams* (2012), and Kirk Honeycutt's *John Hughes: A Life in Film* (2015), as well as numerous articles in newspapers, magazines, and on websites. By the time *Ferris Bueller* was in production, a mere two years after his directorial debut with *Sixteen Candles*, star Matthew Broderick stated that Hughes had become 'the godlike Spielberg figure of teen movies,' which was quoted in Hadley Freeman's *Life Moves Pretty Fast: The Lessons We Learned from Eighties Movies (and Why We Don't Learn Them from Movies Anymore)*, another book that focused much of its attention on Hughes (2016: 159). The stories about him have become somewhat legendary, supported by their frequent retellings in all of these texts, as well as by direct quotes in original sources. While a lengthy biography is the subject of other sources, there are key points of his life that illustrate how the production of *The Breakfast Club* was shaped by its writer and director, demonstrating Hughes's 'gift for synthesizing the demands of a story and the demands of the marketplace' (Carter 1991).

There is no indication in all the Hughes histories that he initially wanted to be a filmmaker, but from a young age, he was a talented and prolific writer. He had artistic leanings, painting and writing throughout high school and college, and even submitted jokes to comedians like Rodney Danger-field and Joan Rivers, showing his long-standing interest in comedy. But reminded of the income disparities between his family (his father did not earn a lot of money) and his neighbors growing up in the wealthy suburbs of Chicago, Hughes decided to apply himself toward a more stable profession. He needed a steady income after he married his high school girlfriend and had children at a young age, so after dropping out of college, he got jobs with advertising companies where he could be creative but also get paid. The early marketing experiences would prove valuable. Hughes would go to focus groups regularly and was able to distill the 'inherent drama' of a product into successful campaigns; in addition, he showed a desire to give the audience what they wanted and to make films that were popular and accessible (Carter 1991). As a demonstration of the concurrent 1980s focus on the importance of marketing, even from his early films like *National Lampoon's Vacation* (Ramis 1983) and carrying through his career into *Pretty in Pink* and beyond, Hughes would rewrite endings if test audiences did not like what they saw (Hughes 2008).

While good experience in and of itself, teaching Hughes the importance of audience tastes and how to write quickly to meet deadlines, his time with advertising companies in Chicago interestingly also led him to his job with the *National Lampoon*, a popular humor magazine based in New York. While working on an ad campaign for Virginia Slims and traveling back and forth for meetings in their offices headquartered in New York City, he would also go to the *Lampoon* offices and sit in the waiting room, hoping someone would take notice. Eventually, they did, and he was hired as a writer and then an editor. His story, 'Vacation '58' published in 1979, about a family's hapless road trip, was popular enough that Warner Bros. bought the rights to it, and Matty Simmons, the publisher of the *Lampoon*, recommended that Hughes adapt the screenplay. His first forays into filmmaking followed soon after; he had a screenwriting credit on the poorly-received sequel to *National Lampoon*'s *Animal House* (Landis 1978) called *Class Reunion* (Miller 1982), and he wrote *National Lampoon's Vacation* (1983) and *Mr. Mom* (Dragoti 1983). Again, these experiences proved influential on

The Breakfast Club; he lost creative control of the scripts and so decided that he would demand to direct the next screenplays he wrote. With little clout and experience, he insisted on this stipulation, even before the successful releases of *Vacation* and *Mr. Mom*. To keep creative control on *The Breakfast Club*, he ended up taking only scale as payment. As he stated, 'I made myself a producer. I had casting approvals. I didn't make any money on it, but I didn't care. This was my baby' (quoted in Smith 1999: 70).

Because of wanting to direct but having little know-how, the next script Hughes wrote was actually called *Detention*, the original name for *The Breakfast Club* (the title of the film was changed later based on what an advertising colleague's son told him they called morning detention at his high school (Smith 1999: 69); Hughes did not think anyone would mind that he applied the label to the whole-day detention of the film). He decided on the story because it primarily took place all in one room, with young actors he thought would not be experienced enough to realize his inexperience, and because it would be inexpensive to produce. Hughes thought it akin to a play and felt comfortable enough with the prospect of directing it, and with having a very brief cameo (see Figure 1.1), even though he would later tell *Entertainment Weekly* that 'I stumbled into this business, I didn't train for it. I yelled "Action!" on my first two movies before the camera was turned on' (Appelo 1994).

Figure 1.1 Hughes's cameo; he stuck to writing, directing, and producing – he was going to have a line, but it was cut because he thought his acting was terrible (Smith 1999: 74).

What Hughes lacked in experience as a filmmaker, he made up for in his talent as a storyteller and in his willingness to learn from people. From early on, Hughes said in an interview that 'I just don't think 16-year-olds are being served well by my generation' (Barth 1984: 46); he made a point of focusing on everyday teenagers and, importantly, on taking them and their problems seriously. It also helped that as a kid himself, Hughes said that he was 'obsessed with romance' (Ringwald 1986), not on the sex-quest *Porky's*-style storylines that were in vogue in the early part of the decade. This proclivity happened to be in line with what the youth marketing research reports indicated teens were interested in seeing. It was also a good fit with his autobiographical writing style; many of the characters he wrote were based on people he knew, but even more than that, many were surrogates for himself or 'refractions and distillations of various parts of a very complex character' (Kamp 2010b). Hughes's own life stories, in their multiple varieties and variations, about romance and about sometimes feeling like an awkward outsider teenager, struck a chord especially with youth audiences who could relate to the experiences.

Hughes did not just use his own life as fodder. He was also known to form very close relationships with people with whom he worked (even though he was equally as well-known for being difficult and for holding long-standing grudges, often against the same people with whom he was once close (Ringwald 2009)). Like someone who was genuinely interested in getting a youth perspective, and like someone who was experienced in advertising and understood the importance of knowing his audience, he mined them for their input. Since he was interested in getting at the – if not exactly authentic then at least relatable – female adolescent experience, he asked Sloane Tanen, the daughter of studio executive and *The Breakfast Club* producer Ned Tanen (and for whom Ferris Bueller's girlfriend was likely named), questions about her life, almost as though she were a one-girl focus group and test audience (Gora 2010: 187). Alison Byrne Fields, a fan who wrote him a letter telling him about how much his films meant to her, also ended up being his confidante and source for market research; they were pen pals for years as he wrote screenplays in the 1980s, and he would sometimes say a film decision he made was for her (Byrne Fields 2009). And of course, Molly Ringwald, the star of three of his films dubbed the 'Molly Trilogy' – *Sixteen Candles*, *The Breakfast Club*, and *Pretty in Pink* (Corliss 1986) – was the teen actress with whom he was closest and whose 'opinion carried more weight' than anyone else's (John Cryer, of *Pretty in Pink*, quoted in Gora 2010: 141). He was not fond just of Ringwald though; he was collaborative with many of his actors and crew, often encouraging them to offer their input during filming.

Ringwald especially served as an inspiration and influence not just during production but during the pre-production writing process as well. Her role as his muse would come into play even before filming began. Hughes was getting some traction with his new *Detention* screenplay. A&M, known primarily as a music label, was starting a film division run by Gil Friesen, and they decided to put up $750,000 for producing *Detention* in 1982 (Honeycutt 2015: 57). In the middle of trying to cast the film, Hughes wrote another script in a matter of days titled *Sixteen Candles*. Throughout his writing burst, he was inspired by the headshot he saw of young Ringwald that he kept tacked above his desk. The two had not met yet though. Getting flashes of ideas, quickly writing screenplays, and being extremely prolific were some of Hughes's famous traits and ones that led to having so many films ready to produce in such rapid succession. In the middle of working on *Detention*, he sent *Sixteen Candles* to the ICM talent agency, and then president Jeff Berg shopped it around on the condition that its writer also direct. Michelle Manning, who would soon become a co-producer on *The Breakfast Club*, had heard executives pass on it at other studios, but when she applied for a new job at Channel Productions and was asked if she knew of any scripts, she recommended Hughes and his teen film (Gora 2010: 23).

The studio executive and producer: Ned Tanen

Probably the person who was the most influential behind the scenes in getting *The Breakfast Club* made was Ned Tanen. Tanen was a legendary executive in Hollywood, at the helm as president first of Universal and then of Paramount when his studios had record-breaking box-office years, and was known for his 'Midas touch in bringing youth-oriented films' to the screen (Grimes 2009). Importantly, he was also known not just to favor youth films but also to champion his talent. He was production vice president and then president of Universal Pictures, where he greenlit successful teen films like *American Graffiti* (Lucas 1973), *Animal House*, and *Fast Times at Ridgemont High* (Heckerling 1982), before he stepped down to form his own film company, Channel Productions, so he could focus more on moviemaking instead of other aspects of the business. It was when he was starting this company that Michelle Manning brought John Hughes to his attention, even though he had actually met him and been impressed by his wit years before when he visited the *Lampoon* offices (Gora 2010: 24).

Because of his position, Tanen had the clout to hire an unknown, and because of his connections – he also knew Friesen at A&M – even though *Detention* was already in pre-production, they agreed to partner on it. However, Tanen wanted to make *Sixteen Candles* first because he thought it was more commercial than a film that was mostly people sitting around talking in one room. Tanen could and did surround first-time filmmaker Hughes with a talented crew, and filming *Sixteen Candles* first would give Hughes some experience with the decidedly more difficult film that would later become *The Breakfast Club*. This was all in line with Tanen's reputation. Sherry Lansing, former CEO of Paramount, said 'he could always spot the talent – his instincts were so good,' and Sean Daniel, former production president of Universal, stated that 'he forced us to take risks while he always had our backs' (Saperstein 2009a). In interviews around the time *The Breakfast Club* was released, Hughes himself noted the huge role Tanen played in getting the film financed and distributed and in protecting him:

> I credit Ned Tanen for reading a script that a lot of people said would make a wonderful play but not a movie . . . And I credit him for seeing it as a movie. I also credit him for seeing me as someone who could direct it. And I credit him for ramming it through the studio system and protecting me. When the studio called me and said, 'It's not funny enough,' I credit him for saying, 'Leave him alone.'
>
> (Siskel 1985b)

Tanen's Channel Productions was the company behind a few youth-oriented films with similar casts and crew released in quick succession in the mid-1980s: *St. Elmo's Fire* and *Pretty in Pink*. While Hughes was still in the middle of editing *The Breakfast Club*, Tanen moved to Paramount, causing a bit of tension. He still protected Hughes and the film during post-production though, notably when he protested the marketing plans of the new studio heads who were trying to release the film as a straight comedy (Smith 1999: 145; Gora 2010: 79). Tanen signed deals with Hughes at Paramount, where they would go on to release *Pretty in Pink* and *Ferris Bueller's Day Off*, but by that point, Hughes was no longer seen as a risk but rather a box-office draw and a filmmaker who could speak to contemporary youth audiences. With Tanen behind the scenes as studio executive and producer, and a talented cast of young actors in front of the camera, *The Breakfast Club* was taking shape.

The cast

Emilio Estevez as Andrew Clark, the jock; Anthony Michael Hall as Brian Johnson, the brain; Judd Nelson as John Bender, the criminal; Molly Ringwald as Claire Standish, the princess; and Ally Sheedy as Allison Reynolds, the basket case (labels from the film; the one-sheet labels for the character types were jock, brain, rebel, beauty, and recluse, respectively); Paul Gleason as Richard Vernon; and John Kapelos as Carl, the janitor

One of the reasons for the prolific production trend of teen films during the 1980s was because there were so many talented young actors in Hollywood at the time. *The Breakfast Club* was being made in the middle of this wave and is one of the films most closely associated with the term 'Brat Pack.' The Brat Pack was a phrase coined by David Blum in an article he wrote for *New York* magazine in 1985, between the releases of *The Breakfast Club* in February and *St. Elmo's Fire* in June (Blum 1985). The author was initially doing a piece on Emilio Estevez, who was considered a rising talent as an actor, screenwriter, and director, and who was friends with and had starred in a few films with other people featured in the piece like Anthony Michael Hall, Rob Lowe, Andrew McCarthy, Demi Moore, Judd Nelson, Molly Ringwald, and Ally Sheedy. A riff on the Rat Pack (a group of actors including Frank Sinatra and Sammy Davis, Jr.), while the term is catchy and increased publicity and awareness, it is also decidedly more derisive than the label that inspired it. Calling the actors the Brat Pack had the effect of diminishing their actual talent and pigeonholing them into certain roles. However, the label made them even more famous and brought lasting recognition to their roles. *The Breakfast Club*, as one of the films that starred a bevy of Brat Packers, benefitted from both the rising fame of its actors and from the reason they were famous in the first place: their talent and appeal.

One of the actors most closely associated with Hughes, the Brat Pack, and *The Breakfast Club* is Molly Ringwald. She became a popular star in the 1980s, appearing on the magazine covers of *Seventeen* but also on *Time* and *Life*, all in 1986, after appearing in three Hughes films in three years. She was labeled a 'muse' for Hughes, especially because of the stories of how he would write screenplays for her and because of their close kinship. After Hughes's death, film critic A. O. Scott in the *New York Times* noted 'Molly Ringwald was for Mr. Hughes what Jimmy Stewart was for Frank Capra: an emblem, a muse, a poster child and an alter-ego' (2009). And at the height of her popularity, critic Pauline Kael said in her review of *Pretty in Pink* that she possessed a 'charismatic normality' (1989), astutely describing the way she was like an especially captivating every-teen, not someone who was an unrealistic ideal, yet someone who had an alluring on-screen presence. She was known for the range of emotions she could express without seeming like she was forcing them and for being mature yet youthful. The 1986 *Time* article by Richard Corliss was full of glowing praises, describing how she could set teens 'queuing at the box office,' how she had 'her own girl groupies' named 'Ringlets' who emulated her style, and how she was 'hip enough to be the style setter of Right Now and traditional enough to be any American teen of the past 50 years.' While Corliss (1986) also noted the 'spectacular ensemble acting' of films starring a 'veritable Hughes' Who' of other actors, Ringwald was the one who seemed to be the biggest draw, especially because of the collaboration and symbiosis with Hughes.

Ringwald was not the only actor who had such a close relationship with Hughes. Anthony Michael Hall, who first appeared in *Vacation*, was also a close compatriot of the director. They too were seen as such an indelible pair that Stanley Kubrick, when trying to cast Hall in the roll of Joker in *Full Metal Jacket* (1987), initially compared Hughes to Frank Capra but Hall to James Stewart (Kamp 2010b). Figuring as another surrogate for one of the many aspects of Hughes's life, Hall exemplified the geeky outsider teen with a sense of humor and earnestness. He also had keen comic timing and, like many of the other actors with whom Hughes worked, was known for improvising. Indeed, Hughes was extremely generous with his actors and was not precious about keeping every word of dialogue as written. Howard Deutch, who cut the trailer for *The Breakfast Club* and then later went on to direct *Pretty in Pink*, stated, 'I've never seen a writer who is so willing to adapt his dialogue and script' (Corliss 1986), and Ringwald stated, 'If you wanted to change something or make it your own, John completely encouraged it' (Kamp 2010a). Hughes found, in both Ringwald and Hall, actors he could mentor and befriend and talent that would add even more genuine characterization to his screenplays.

Jackie Burch was hired as the casting director for *The Breakfast Club*, and even though Hughes already knew he wanted Ringwald and Hall (Smith 1999: 70) and while there was some pre-production headway made while the film was at A&M before *Sixteen Candles*, the other roles still needed to be filled. Ally Sheedy, who was coming off starring in *WarGames* (Badham 1983), had read for a part in *Sixteen Candles* and tells of how she had two black eyes from an accident on set the day before her audition (72); Hughes remembered her, and although there are still rumors about which female role she would play, the basket case was the better fit. Emilio Estevez, who had recently starred in *The Outsiders* (Coppola 1983), another successful box-office teen film, came in to read and originally wanted the role of the rebel but was cast as the jock instead (Honeycutt 2015: 68). The criminal/rebel character was the hardest to fill and was the last one to be cast in the final iteration. John Cusack, who had had a small part in *Sixteen Candles*, was hired initially, but Burch didn't think he was menacing enough. She brought in Judd Nelson for the part; he came in character to the audition and was almost thrown out of the building. He was so dedicated to playing his role that, in the method acting style, he stayed in character during the first part of production and was almost fired because Hughes did not like how he was treating Ringwald when they were not filming. Nelson subsequently toned down his off-screen behavior and kept the part (Smith 1999: 76). The film was dialogue-heavy and action-light, so choosing the best actors to achieve the right ensemble dynamic was essential. Because of the 1980s timing, there was a pool of talented young actors from which they could choose.

Aside from the parents who drop their kids off at the beginning of the film (and Hughes who played Hall's character's father at the end), there were only two other adult roles with any significant screen time. Hughes remembered finding Paul Gleason funny in his part in *Trading Places* (Landis 1983), and he was cast as Vernon because of both his humor and adversarial stance. Meanwhile, the janitor was a later add-on. In line with 1980s teen sex romps and pressure from the studio to make the film more commercial, originally there was supposed to be a scene of a topless swim instructor taking a shower (Honeycutt 2015: 74). In the spirit of the collaborative nature of the filmmaking process and how open Hughes was to suggestions, one night when Hughes had the cast and co-producer Michelle Manning over for one of the dinners he would host at his house during production, this role was changed. Ringwald, Sheedy, and Manning thought the scenes were gratuitous, and Hughes agreed, so instead of a swim instructor, he wrote in the part of Carl, the janitor. Originally, Rick Moranis was cast and played the role with broad comedy and a Russian accent; since this didn't mesh with the rest of the film, the part was re-cast with John Kapelos, who had a part as Ringwald's character's brother-in-law in *Sixteen Candles* (Smith 1999: 74; Honeycutt 2015: 76).

Interestingly, this version of events is contested by Karen Leigh Hopkins (2015), the actress cast as the swim instructor, who said she never read or filmed a nude scene and thought she was there to 'bridge the gap between the students and the establishment,' a character more akin to what Carl's eventually was. While what actually happened when is uncertain, ultimately, the adult characters are there to complement and advance the teens' development. Additionally, finding the right tone, a balance between the dramatic and the comedic, and extending this to the casting of the adult roles, was in line with the larger vision for the film.

As the production histories detailed in Smith (1999), Gora (2010), and Honeycutt (2015) all attest, the collaborative filmmaking style helped impart a sense of cohesiveness to and comfort between the actors. Hughes fostered this environment and was a part of it himself. The actors stayed together in the same hotel while filming, and the film was shot on location in Chicago instead of near the usual haunts and familiar faces they might otherwise be around in Hollywood, further enhancing the bonds of the group. Hughes, who lived close to the no-longer-in-use high school where they filmed, would joke around with the cast after filming, have some of the cast and crew over for dinner at his house, take them out to Chicago, and make them mix tapes from his extensive music collection. When filming, he would check the camera angle and then move away from behind the camera to sit next to the camera in order to be closer to the cast. Hughes let the cameras roll, capturing multiple takes and encouraging different ways to play the scenes. Because the film was shot in sequence, the characters and relationships developed as filmmaking progressed.

To further enhance the camaraderie, Hughes used the time while the set was being built to have an extensive rehearsal period of almost three weeks before shooting began (Smith 1999: 72). Trying to get at a sense of realism and to help the actors get a feel for their characters, on top of basing characters on people he knew, he had Estevez and Nelson go 'undercover' in a local high school and hang out in the halls where their respective characters would (ibid.). While the actors improvised lines, he also encouraged them to contribute in other creative and quite substantive areas – they decided that their characters would be sitting at different tables instead of one and thought of where specifically they would each sit (Honeycutt 2015: 74). Such a detail, especially because they were going to be in that room for most of the day, has a huge impact on the overall film (see Figure 1.2). Marilyn Vance, the costume designer who came up with vision boards for what each character would wear, originally had more princess-like outfits picked out for the princess, but Ringwald thought the character should look more sophisticated and demanding instead of frilly and childish (Smith 1999: 76; Honeycutt 2015: 79). During rehearsals, when Hughes told the actors he had multiple previous drafts of the script, the actors asked to see the other versions and ended up cherry-picking parts they thought worked (Smith 1999: 72). Sheedy even

Figure 1.2 Overhead shot of the library, with the characters separated.

recommended the David Bowie song 'Changes' to Hughes, a quote from which opens the film (Gora 2010: 162). The cast was emboldened by this freedom and empowered by the value placed on their ideas. Hughes thought it was important to tell the story of everyday teens living regular lives, and having the young cast have so much input added legitimacy and depth to the way they inhabited their roles and to the overall film.

Additional crew: Thomas Del Ruth (cinematographer) and Dede Allen (editor)

Aside from having little experience as a director, Hughes's burgeoning film-making style itself posed a few challenges. Notably, because he had a long script, because he let the camera keep rolling as the actors tried different approaches, and because of the ensemble nature of the film where he wanted to get multiple characters in one shot, there ended up being over a million feet of film shot during the thirty-two-day shoot, with 200,000 alone taken of the final 'group therapy' scene at the end (Smith 1999: 74; Honeycutt 2015: 77) (see Figures 1.3 and 1.4). Another challenge was that Ringwald and Hall were both younger than eighteen, meaning there were restrictions on how many hours they could work on set because of child labor laws. Scenes had to be shot multiple times to accommodate their schedules. Cinematographer Thomas Del Ruth stated that they 'tried to include all of the kids in all of the shots, because it was the group that was working their

Figure 1.3 The 'group therapy' session at the end, with all the characters together.

Figure 1.4 The 'therapy' scene took almost 20 minutes of screen time, allowing for tonal shifts.

way through life, not the individuals. We had hundreds of setups. We never shot one piece of dialogue from only one angle' (quoted in Smith 1999: 74). When Hughes sat on the floor to be closer to the cast, Del Ruth was the one behind the camera. There was so much footage in fact, and so many different takes where Hughes would just have the camera keep rolling until it ran out of film, that eventually Bob Forrest, the script supervisor, stopped taking notes and starting using a recorder. Exasperated with the shoot, he left in the middle of filming and apparently retired after *The Breakfast Club* (Smith 1999: 74).

In detailing Hughes's impact on filmmaking even before he died in 2009, the *Los Angeles Times* ran a piece about the influence of Hughes's style of having the actors try scenes multiple ways while continuing to record. Tom Jacobson, a producer who spent a decade working on various Hughes projects, said the writer/director

> loved his actors and loved language, so he'd shoot a lot of film . . . It became a big thing in comedy after John did it – listening to the actors and looking for those great moments. John would hear a line and get the actor to go with it. It really wasn't the actors who were improvising. It was John improvising.

> (quoted in Goldstein 2008)

While this helped in getting the right tone and capturing just the right moments, it also meant a tremendous amount of footage that needed to be managed and made coherent.

In addition to supporting Hughes with the studio, Ned Tanen made sure to surround him with more experienced talent. One of the most significant hires in this regard was probably Dede Allen, the veteran and well-respected film editor who cut *Bonnie and Clyde* (Penn 1967), *Serpico* (Lumet 1973), and *Reds* (Beatty 1981). Allen was working with Hughes in Chicago during production, not just editing during post-production. Because there was so much footage and such a high shooting ratio, there were some nights that it took almost an hour go through the dailies, and in fact the rough cut of the film was almost three hours long (the final theatrical version was 97 minutes). Allen would go through the footage and impart some important lessons to Hughes about keeping only what was essential. Hughes said he learned from Allen that 'nothing matters so much as communicating what a character is' (quoted in Honeycutt 2015: 77), reinforcing how paramount the teens' story was. Allen also contributed to the actual production process; she would recommend what shots she still needed in order to make the film less stagnant. When talking about *The Breakfast Club*, Allen stated that 'it was an awful lot of footage that was pretty static. You had to beat it a lot to make it dance' (quoted in Smith 1999: 145). That the final film does not feel like a filmed version of a stage play is largely a credit to Allen's and Hughes's collaboration.

Between the state of the larger Hollywood industry with its focus on the youth market and the cast and crew that was available at the time, *The Breakfast Club* came together as a product of multiple opportune circumstances. Of course, even with an industry in the middle of tumultuous upheaval because of the introduction of new technologies, changes in corporate structure, and shifting business strategies, and even with a market primed for more teen films because of recent popular titles and because of trying to appeal to the important youth demographic, there was no guarantee that this particular film would be a hit. And even though the film was largely the brainchild of someone who would go on to be a hugely successful filmmaker and had contributions from the tremendous talent assembled, at the time, the film itself was considered a risk. Consisting of primarily five troubled teens sitting in a room talking, what it lacked in action, it made up for in character. Before the film was released, Hughes himself said,

> My best guess is that it will do well . . . But I told the actors that if 'Breakfast Club' bombs, we have nothing to be ashamed of I said, 'We have made a movie that will be around for a long time. If nothing else,

even if it doesn't do any business, we have documented a slice of life that normally doesn't get documented in the movies. It will live on cassettes; it will live on television. We can be proud of this.'

(quoted in Siskel 1985b)

That *The Breakfast Club* did turn out to be affecting has to do with what the film is about and the way it is told, but industrial factors and key personnel were instrumental to laying the foundation for its success.

2 Rules of the genre

Creating iconic characters while breaking down stereotypes

When trying to assess how a film creates meaning, how it fits into a genre, how it works, and why it is so significant, one of the main areas of focus is on analyzing the film text itself. The importance of the context of production of *The Breakfast Club* is essential for understanding how and why it was such a significant film – the historical context, in terms of what was going on in the country and in the film industry at the time it was made, gives a broader background for understanding what issues the film touches upon and the meaning imparted as a result. But textual analysis reveals the content, what the film actually does and says, how it fits into and comments upon the larger teen film genre, and explains why *The Breakfast Club* remains so canonical. The two together, the content and the context, the text itself and its frameworks, can explain its larger and lasting significance.

As Rick Altman (2012 (1984), 1999) states, genres and genre films can be identified by a semantic and syntactic approach where the semantic, like words of a language, refers to the things we can see in the film, such as the iconography, characters, and settings, and the syntactic, like the grammatical rules of a sentence, refers to the ways the elements are organized, to the recurring organizational structures and relationships between them. By pointing out the iconography of *The Breakfast Club*, including the five main characters, the adults, the costumes and props, the high school setting, etc., we get a sense of what a teen film looks like and of the visual elements that we come to expect when we see a film of this genre. By studying the relationships between these components, including how the characters interact and the struggles that are overcome, we get a sense of the rules of the film and how it functions as part of the teen film genre as a whole. Looking at the series of relationships between the elements, such as the conflicts between youth and authority figures, the story elements of the teens fighting and celebrating with one another, and the themes of pressure and self-acceptance, reveals how the coming-of-age process depicted in *The Breakfast Club* speaks to the generation growing up at the time and to the more universal, timeless issues surrounding this fraught period of life.

Another way to examine a film through the lens of genre is to think of the text as having multiple layers. On a surface level, when we think of genre films, we can identify them as 'films which, through repetition and variation, tell familiar stories with familiar characters in familiar situations' (Grant 2003: xv). On a deeper level, though, genres function as coded systems, and by revealing those codes, often uncovered by looking at the relationships of elements that are set in opposition to one another, the individual genre films try to deal with and find solutions to enduring cultural conflicts and contradictions that often do not have easy real-world answers (Schatz 1981: 263). Following the theories posed by Claude Levi-Strauss and Roland Barthes, Thomas Schatz notes that the repetition of certain stories can be seen as part of a mythic structure; the stories are told again and again because they represent problems in society that can never be fully resolved and so are repeated as in a ritual to provide comfort. Although surface changes are meaningful and keep films of the genre relevant to contemporary audiences, the basic underlying principles of the form remain intact. Studying genre films in this way is thus a useful model for blending theoretical and historical approaches. For the teen film, this can be seen with identifying the oppositions between youth and authority, but it is also borne out in the oppositions between, for example, feeling normal vs. different, like an outsider vs. an insider, where what signifies difference and what is popular shift over time. Additional ideas are signaled by this proposition: using structural methods of textual analysis can reveal underlying principles of how a text works, how it relates to the genre of which it is a part, and how it connects to culture and society.

Still an additional method of genre analysis that relies on examining the textual components of the film is to look at the way the film fits into the evolution of the genre on a larger scale. Schatz (1981), as well as John Cawelti (1979) and Altman (1999), discuss the ways genres develop and have a cycle composed of different stages where early on the genre is developing, in the middle it is maturing, and later on it becomes self-aware and reflexive. While the stages are fluid and the models are contested, it is still a useful framework to illustrate how genres can be compared to a life cycle of sorts. When films display elements of reflexivity, or a self-awareness of themselves as texts that operate in the teen film genre mode, it is indicative of a genre with rules that have been codified, with ways it operates that audiences have over time come to expect and understand. *The Breakfast Club* acknowledges the constructed nature of stereotypes but stops short of parody or satire of the form, showing that the teen film, in a period of maturation, was becoming an established genre and, as such, was addressing contemporary, relevant issues.

Following these analytical frameworks, this chapter proceeds by examining the surface textual elements and how story and themes reveal the governing relationships between those constituent parts. Then, to show how 'inherent dramatic conflicts represent its most basic determining feature' (Schatz 1981: 31), the film's central narrative oppositions are investigated, namely the conflicts between youth and authority, between different peer groups, and within the teens themselves as individuals. Finally, after discussing how the constituent parts of the film work together, the analysis shifts to examining how the text fits into the development of the teen film genre. Looking at the semantics and syntactics of *The Breakfast Club*, next at the central narrative conflicts, and then at the way the film is a step in the evolution of the form reveals themes in the text itself, the genre as a whole, and the culture at large.

Semantics and syntactics: iconography and characters, story and theme

Some of the most obvious textual elements of a film are the visual objects, characters, and plot. Simply put in terms of its surface level, *The Breakfast Club* is about five high school students in detention. As a starting point then, one of the apparent indicators of genre, especially at the height of certain actors' popularity, is the casting. In the case of *The Breakfast Club*, the personnel in front of the screen, as well as John Hughes behind it, signal a teen film. Even though only Anthony Michael Hall and Molly Ringwald were teens at the time of production while Emilio Estevez, Judd Nelson, and Ally Sheedy were in their 20s, they were all part of a group of actors eventually known as the Brat Pack, after David Blum labeled them as such in a *New York* magazine article in 1985. The so-called 'pack' of actors often worked together in different combinations during the decade, and the films they appeared in were predominantly either teen or youth-oriented.

While casting is a shorthand way of identifying genre, iconography and setting are others that are also imbued with meaning. In the teen film, youth often exist in spaces where they are supposed to be monitored (although rarely are) or where they are left unsupervised and have to take care of themselves. One of the locations that most often signifies a teen film is the high school. Usually set in the suburbs, it is the place where mostly teens (although older educators too) spend a great deal of time. High schools are where teens 'work' – where they are supposed to learn and prepare for their futures in college or in a job. These parts of their education, however, are often overshadowed in films by the socialization purposes schools serve.

Learning how to navigate through different social situations is usually a more important focus of the narratives than academics, as is the case with *The Breakfast Club*.

While they serve as learning grounds of multiple sorts, high schools can also serve as a microcosm for the larger communities in which the teens reside. Often as people get older, their regular social associations are with individuals who share similarities, even though they still have some interactions with those who are different. In high schools, however, teens can mix with people from a range of social strata, classes, and educational levels. These social interactions with people who are different from them happen less in academic classes segmented by aptitude or in friend groups students choose. But the places where various groups congregate, like school halls, locker rooms, cafeterias, and grounds can often be sites of conflict. These spaces of unsegregated congregation are laden with danger, especially when the teens are left unsupervised. In *The Breakfast Club*, this type of situation is accentuated by having the teens from different educational, class, and social groups forced together in one room in the library for the entire day of detention. The different physical spaces in the school the characters usually occupy are reconstructed by the places where the characters sit. At the beginning of the day, Andy and Claire, the two who would seem to have the closest association because of their popularity in the school, sit at the same table in the front. The others locate themselves at their own tables, and noticeably the 'cool' kids sit on one side of the room while the ones who are not according to the school classifications (Brian and Allison) sit on the other. As the day progresses, their seating positions change to reflect the ways they have become closer and on a similar level with one another, to the eventual point where they all sit on the floor together in a circle (see Figures 1.3 and 1.4).

The majority of the film takes place in the library, but other settings are used as well. Vernon, the teacher supposedly in charge of monitoring the teens, occasionally comes into the library but mostly stays in his nearby office, the halls, or in the basement records room. He occupies the spaces that surround and undergird the students, lurking as a menace and establishing a foundation for the authoritative rules of the high school. When he locks Bender in a storage room, it is as though he is trying to hide away and contain a threat he cannot control in the recesses of the building where detritus is thrown. Of course, he is unsuccessful, as the room is still accessible via the air ducts Bender crawls though and what is assumed the hallway Claire braves to get to him at the end of the day. Notably, in the beginning and end of the film, four of the students' parents appear in front of the school, never themselves entering the teen space, even though their influence permeates the boundaries through the teens' thoughts and behaviors. Using Christopher

Vogler's (2007) breakdown of the hero's journey, which builds on Joseph Campbell's analysis of mythic structure, the outside of the building and even the main area of the library can be seen as the regular world the teens occupy and the hallways the thresholds, while the library's interior spaces and the alcoves off to the sides are the special world, or the inmost cave, where the teens achieve their quests on their journeys of development. It is in these recesses of the library where they gain enough confidence to reveal their true identities and, in the process, really see and bond with one another.

Still more settings are occupied or merely indicated in the film, and although these locations and the props associated with them are only seen briefly, they reveal telling associations. During Brian's first voiceover, shots of spaces accompany the letter he reads to Vernon – the clock marking the time, the halls, and the cafeteria, and then shots that we learn later have more significance: a locker with the door blown off and charred contents spilling out are likely Brian's locker after the flair gun went off; a wrestler, perhaps Andy, is on the cover of the student newspaper; there is graffiti on walls and garbage in the corners where Bender and his friends might hang out; an open composition notebook with the word 'help' written over and over again is a nod to Allison's mental state; and as a bit of irony and well-integrated exposition, Carl the janitor's senior portrait shows that he was 'Man of the Year' in 1969. As Brian reads off the character types, more associations are made between the corresponding settings and props: the brain and the computer room, the athlete and the messy gym locker room, the basket case and a counselor's office, the princess and a banner telling students to vote for their prom queen, and the criminal and a camera tilt downward along a locker with a noose warning people to stay out. The high school iconography of these opening shots, along with the different types of cars the parents drive and the costumes the teens wear (plain brown jacket and a beanie, varsity letter jacket, bulky dark parka, expensive leather jacket, trench coat and sunglasses), serve as a shorthand way to give socioeconomic status and social strata information about character.

As a result of these labels and associations, each of the five teens is initially perceived to be easily understood and known by their surface qualities, such as their costumes and the spaces they usually inhabit, because they are being purposefully categorized as stereotypes. That these stereotypes are clearly labeled as such reveals a text ripe for structural analysis – the stereotyped characters are archetypes that stand in for teen characters at large, for types that are common to teens both in the real world and in teen films.

> Indeed, archetypes are themselves structural in nature: in order to be an archetype, an image, character type, or other narrative element must serve as a structural model that generates numerous different versions

of itself, that is, numerous different surface phenomena with the same underlying structure.

(Tyson 2015: 211)

The archetypes represented are some of the most common of the stock characters that populate high schools and the teen film genre: popular kids (Claire), jocks (Andy), rebels (Bender), nerds/geeks (Brian), and outcasts (Allison), with all the different types usually in conflict with one another because of the groups to which they belong. Other stock characters that commonly appear in the genre, such as first loves and crushes, bullies, projects (Pygmalion types), and partiers, also have attributes that overlap with the five in *The Breakfast Club*.

Interestingly, revealing nuances of the stereotypes does not minimize the function of archetypes in the teen film. Instead, by pointing out the stereotypical nature of the archetypes, by showing them to be more than mere caricatures, they are made more complex; they are made to more clearly tie their filmic representation to their real-life counterparts. If the film can reveal that teens, and that specific types of teens who are grouped into categories because of what they do or because of who their friends are, are actually individuals, then it speaks to real teens being treated as whole human beings. Instead of labeling, and then discarding, teen characters as flat or lacking depth, or as young adults either just in process of being indoctrinated into society or as troublemakers with no hope for the future, they are made more multifaceted. All people can be classified with simplicity. If we get to know them, which is predicated upon wanting to get to know them in the first place, then we understand that everyone has his and her own sets of problems. Even though the film for the most part does not go beyond stereotypical representations of authority figures, what *The Breakfast Club* does do is provide insight into teens – not only does it lay out the rules of the teen social and class systems, gender norms, and family dynamics, but it then complicates them to reveal that many of the differences between characters are on the surface, while the similarities are deeper than previously thought. That the characters are similar does not mean they are all the same; rather, it means that some of their problems are universal and relatable. Revealing specific details of the archetypical characters complicates the stereotypes and in so doing, gives greater depth and complexity to their recurring representations in the teen film.

Showing how the stereotypes are foregrounded and then broken down gets at the central plot lines and thematic elements of *The Breakfast Club*. Again, in basic terms, the film is about five high school students from different social circles who all have to serve a full Saturday of detention together. As the film progresses, more of the story and characters are revealed. Even though they can each be categorized as a stereotype, as they talk, fight, get high, and actually learn more about one another, they realize there is more to all of them, that it was wrong to think they knew each other before the day started because of their labels. They realize they all have serious problems at home and at school and are each under tremendous pressure, be it to succeed in academics or sports; to deal with parents who use, abuse, or ignore them; or to live up to standards and expectations from their friends. While there may be exterior differences between them, they all share an animosity toward their common adversaries – their parents and the teachers at school – and all experience the very real fear that those authority figures pose threats for them all. They realize, as Andy states, that 'we're all pretty bizarre. Some of us are just better at hiding it, that's all.'

The five become friends over the course of the day as they reveal more about themselves and why they are in detention. But the question lingers about whether they will be able to overcome the powerful peer pressure they feel among their usual friends. They do not know if their social groups will approve or how much this approval will still matter to them when they are back in their everyday world. Thematically, the film shows how teens can at once be self-aware and confused, empowered and challenged. One of the things that sets *The Breakfast Club* apart, even though it is such a canonical genre film representative of the form, is that there remains this ambiguity about the ending. It is not clear whether the five will remain friends on Monday, how long the romances will last, or exactly what Bender's fist pump of triumph at the end is for. There is, however, a sense of catharsis when watching the film; it feels as though something has been accomplished by watching the teens learn about one another and connect, stand up for themselves and decide who they want to be, and reach self-acceptance and confidence. The ambiguous ending speaks to the sense of realism the film achieves by presenting rounded teenaged characters in relatable situations. By containing uncertainty, the film also points to an emblematic nature of genres – they temporarily address and resolve real-world problems that cannot actually be answered so easily outside mythic/filmic representations. We may have hopes for how things will turn out, and we may want positive change and idealism to last, but we do not know for sure, and we cannot know what the future holds. By grounding and giving depth to the portrayal of the five once stereotypical characters and by depicting the various enduring conflicts they face, the film is both a model of the genre and exemplary of the ways teens come of age.

Narrative oppositions: youth against authority, peer groups, and their inner selves

While the analysis of the semantics and syntactics illustrates that the teens are all individuals facing similar problems, an analysis of the dominant narrative conflicts reveals just how those similarities play out. The dominant conflicts of the film can be revealed by looking at repeated binary oppositions – textual elements that are set against one another. According to Claude Lévi-Strauss (1963), myths work as a kind of sign system, where, like a language, one thing stands for something else. A way to understand how these sign systems create and impart meaning is to analyze how they work on their fundamental level, or their deep structure. Borrowing from theoretical ideas in cultural anthropology and linguistics, this underlying structure can be revealed by noting a series of oppositions. Applying a structural framework to *The Breakfast Club* reveals a number of oppositional elements that in turn identify the central ways in which the film produces meaning. Highlighting these oppositions then leads to a greater understanding of how the film addresses and constructs the coming-of-age process depicted in the teen film genre.

One of the most notable, overarching binaries in *The Breakfast Club*, and indeed in teen films more generally, is the opposition between youth and authority figures. The more specific structural elements of this overarching opposition are borne out by noting differences between young/old, past/future, and even safety/danger. *The Breakfast Club* depicts this bundle of oppositions primarily by showing the conflicts between the teens and Vernon, the teacher responsible for overseeing them during detention. Vernon does not understand the teens in his charge and cannot relate to them. He is constantly trying to assert his authority by yelling at them, comparing himself to a bull and saying that if they mess with him, they will get his horns, and eventually, clearly illustrating the safety/danger opposition adults and improperly supervised spaces pose, by threatening Bender with physical violence, daring him to start a fight so that he could beat up a high schooler whom no one would believe was not the one at fault. Because he is such an adversarial presence, the teens, even though they do not like one another that much especially at the beginning of the film, like Vernon even less. As a result, they join together in a united front of defiance against him, covering for Bender when he takes the hinges off the library door and when he makes a 'ruckus' falling through the ceiling (see Figure 2.1). Vernon is an example of an authority figure who, even though he chose a career working in a high school, has forgotten, or maybe never knew, what it is like to be young. Instead of being a mentor figure, he symbolizes the dichotomies between young and old, represents a sad future, and is just another person the teens have to fight against.

While it is all too easy to villainize Vernon and strip him of the respect he craves but does not command, it is hard to remember that Vernon is in detention too (Christie 2012: 90) and is presented as another stereotyped character who, unlike the teens, is not revealed to be particularly sympathetic. While his behavior is immature and inexcusably reprehensible, it is also a bit more nuanced upon further inspection. As Jan

Figure 2.1 Andy, Brian, and Claire cover for Bender after he falls through the ceiling; meanwhile, Bender is assaulting Claire as he hides under the table.

Chaney points out in 'The Adult Sympathies of *The Breakfast Club*,' that the adults remain stereotypes is by design because the film is not about them, but rather 'it's about the kids, and how they see the world' (2015). However, Chaney also notes that Vernon and Carl's conversation in the records room is revealing and that what they do, say, and feel is somewhat analogous to what the teens upstairs do, say, and feel (or at least the divide between them is not so wide). They are altering their mental states by drinking alcohol just as the teens are smoking marijuana, and Vernon is at heart insecure while Carl seems to have it all figured out. When Vernon tells of his fears that in the future, 'these kids are going to take care of me' and Carl replies, 'I wouldn't count on it,' the exchange expresses a fear common between the adults and the teens, 'that no one cares about them, and that no one ever will' (ibid.). However, less than showing how these particular concerns make Vernon teen-like as Chaney states, it suggests that these fears are more universal to the human condition, regardless of whether the person is young or old. That the teens are mostly excused for their behavior as a result of trying to win admiration from others but Vernon is not is a testament to the idea that adults should know and act better than teenagers but often do not.

The other set of authority figures the teens are set in opposition to are their parents. Even though they are mostly absent, seen only briefly at the beginning and end of the film, and are barely characters unto themselves, the impact they have on their children is tremendous. The parents are universally presented as flawed and as putting their own needs before their kids' needs, wants, and feelings. As a result of the way the parents treat the teens, it appears as if they do not actually care about their children as complete individuals unto themselves; they just see them as a way to live out their own dreams and lost youth (Andy), use them to get back at the other spouse in divorce battles (Claire), put enormous amounts of pressure on them to succeed (Brian and Andy), outright abuse them physically and emotionally (Bender), and ignore them (Allison). The teens then feel that in addition to having to endure difficulties at school, they also have to survive their parents, and they have to do so on their own because to them, no one else understands what they have to live through.

When the teens are sitting on the floor at the group therapy session scene at the end, they notice that they are fighting, hurting, and yelling at one another, just as their parents do, and wonder if they are going to end up like their parents. Even with proclamations of 'not me,' Allison says that it is unavoidable because 'when you grow up, your heart dies.' The teens' future as adults also remains a question at the end of the film, but as they are in the present, they want to believe that they will never use, abuse, and ignore their kids; will never put so much pressure on them that they will be driven to hurt others or themselves as a result; and will never not understand what their kids are going through. Of course, we do not see the teens as adults, just as we do not see what happens on Monday, but we also never see the adults as teens. It is reasonable to guess that if any more of the parents' characters were revealed beyond their stereotypical depictions, they too would be better understood. But again, this film is not about the parents as complete people; it is about understanding the world from the perspective of the particularly astute teens, about seeing what the effects of the parents' actions are, not about seeing the causes of those actions. As a result, there is no alignment between the teens and their parents, and the oppositions between youth/authority and young/old are further reinforced.

Whether there are any sympathetic adults in the teens' world is questionable, but the one who comes the closest to indicating that there can be some détente with the teens is Carl, the janitor. Importantly, he does not hold that much authority over the teens, even though he does tell them that he is the eyes and ears of the school, indicating that they should watch out for him. But there is a not-so-subtle hierarchy he symbolizes – Brian, one of the five who is lower on the popularity totem pole, is embarrassed about acknowledging his friendly relationship with Carl in front of the 'cool' kids, and when Carl says 'hello' to him, Bender makes fun of Brian for it. Later on, as an indication that Brian and Bender have learned something during the day, they both acknowledge Carl when they are leaving. Even though it is ironic that Carl was 'Man of the Year' when he was in high school and now he is a janitor, he is well-adjusted and self-confident, and he cares much less than Vernon about trying to prove his worth and power over the students. When he tells the five he is the eyes and ears, he is somewhat joking, and he gives a knowing smile in response to the greetings he gets. Still, for all his confidence, the fact that he is a janitor does show the dichotomy between another pair of binary oppositions in the teen film, that of past/future. He may have had a different set of prospects when he was in high school, but being a janitor is supposed to illustrate that he did not live up to what people thought he might achieve and that he never left the place where he had attained some glory in the past, demonstrating that in essence, teens' futures are not completely dictated by who they are in high school. He also shows how just because certain people are not held in high regard by societal norms does not mean that they cannot still be fine with themselves regardless of what others may think (and vice versa), one of the essential tenets *The Breakfast Club* espouses.

Even though Carl and Vernon are granted a little bit of complexity and depth, as much time as the film takes to break down stereotypes, it does not really do so with the adult characters. This may be a blind spot, or it could be further indication of the primary perspective the film takes, that of telling a youth story from a youth point of view. Or as Stephen Prince says about Hughes in his larger examination of the 1980s, adults are 'properly distanced from the ideals, longings, and shenanigans' of youth (2000: 212). Whether it is accurate or not, often teens view adults as ones who just do not understand what they are going through and who cannot relate.

However, this reasoning remains a bit too easy: if almost all the blame is on authority figures, what about the self? So much of the teen film genre is about teens coming of age – figuring out who they are and who they want to be now and for the future is a large part of that – but it is also about teens realizing that they have power to decide how to live their lives. Importantly, this comes with learning to take responsibility for their actions. While it is certainly helpful to understand what some of the motivations for their actions are, laying the blame squarely on others for all the negative parts of their lives is in itself somewhat childish. Because the five are articulate and appear mature, it is easy to forget that they are still kids, that they are still coming to terms with life being unfair and confusing, and that the reasons they give for their behaviors may be explanations, even if they see them as excuses.

Authority figures are not the only ones with whom the teens are in conflict though. Another central binary in the teen film and in *The Breakfast Club* is between youth and other members of their peer group. This is underscored by the oppositions in the film most notably between inside/outside but also between carelessness/responsibility and innocence/knowledge. These conflicts are illustrated in the ways the five teens interact with one another throughout the Saturday in detention and in how they and their larger social groups of friends relate to one another during regular school days.

One of their conversations is particularly illustrative of the opposition between inside and outside. During the group therapy session at the end of the film, Brian asks the others whether they think they will still be friends on Monday. Claire's response, although harsh, encapsulates the realities of social hierarchies in the school at the time. She says that it is unlikely that they will remain friends, that her and Andy's friends are the ones Brian and his friends look up to. While Brian would be eager to continue the relationships because he felt a genuine connection to the others, it would also elevate him in some way; however, Claire would not be eager to do so because her friends would look down on her if she did. She knows that the pressure to conform, as much as she hates doing so, might prove too great for her; to maintain her status, her group must be exclusive, and she cannot be seen associating with kids who are not also popular; otherwise, she might then be ostracized by her own clique. The same is true for Bender, Claire states after he criticizes her for being false, because he too is popular, but with a different group of rebellious teens who would not accept a friendship with an outsider, especially one who was a nerd or geek. Claire calls him out on this and tells him he might say 'hello' to Brian to his face but would then make fun of him after he walked away to retain his reputation with his friends. Allison, meanwhile, states that she does not have any friends so there would be no one whose opinions she would care to impress – amusing, but hardly a tenable solution.

The comments about a totem pole of social hierarchies illustrates that teen socialization is not just about whether someone has friends, but it is also about who those friends are and what is necessary to achieve and maintain the status quo. Claire is fashionable and rich, Andy is an athlete, Bender is a rebel – all these impart qualities of an ephemeral 'cool' label. Meanwhile Brian is a nerd, and Allison is 'weird,' and both are part of groups marked as 'others.' While what is cool and popular shifts over time, one thing that it is predicated upon is exclusivity – if everyone is popular, then the label loses its meaning. Only a select few can be part of the elite groups that others admire, that others want to be a part of but cannot. If a group is exclusive, it is both about restricting membership and about keeping others out, about setting people apart from one another in a teen version of the 'haves and have nots.'

The inside/outside dichotomy in this way also relates to the opposition between carelessness/responsibility when examining the ways youth relate to their peers. The teens will do things they think will impress their friends or those they admire in order to cement relationships, even if that means they go against their values or shirk their responsibilities. They know they could be punished if they get caught, but they decide to lie for Bender when he takes the screw from the door, when they go to Bender's locker, when four of them smoke marijuana together, and even when they all agree to have Brian write the essay for them, those moments of having fun and bonding (or getting out of having to do work) are more important than the possible consequences.

Taking risks and having fun, though, sometimes comes at someone else's expense. Just as at the beginning of the day, the five would rather band together against Vernon even though they do not like one another, members of groups ostracize those they want to keep out; however, this bonding and joking can also take a much crueler turn, such as when Andy pulls the locker room prank. Although he blames his father for pressuring him, pressure to be tough and mean in front of his friends also played a part. At the time he 'taped Larry Lester's buns together,' he and his friends were laughing instead of thinking about the ramifications both for themselves and the person they hurt. Some socialization processes take place by affiliating with certain groups and disassociating from others; unfortunately, this is sometimes done by being cruel – if you are mean to someone, that person is set apart so you can align yourself more closely with your supposed allies in an 'us against them' mindset. This further reinforces the differences between being an insider and an outsider, and it sheds a different light on the careless things people do to be accepted. Although this process is certainly not unique to adolescents, it is a prominent, recurring structural element of the teen film.

Peer pressure and the conflict between individuals and the groups of which they are a part also play out in the opposition between innocence/knowledge when thinking about the two romantic relationships formed between Bender and Claire and Andy and Allison. While the binary between innocence/ knowledge is often applied in teen films to those who are virgins and those who are not, the difference is not only about sex. Innocence/knowledge also relates quite literally to not having information and then learning something and, importantly, is about knowing what to do with this newfound knowledge. For the teen film, this can be a question of whether one can hold on to a sense of youthful idealism after learning more about how the world works, about who people really are. In *The Breakfast Club*, the two romantic couples that form and the question about whether they will continue highlight these ideas of attaining knowledge and how to use it in the face of challenges between youth and their peer groups. While Bender and Claire might get together because they realize they were attracted to each other or because they want to anger authority, Andy and Allison's relationship seems to be because of a more genuine connection – Andy showed his interest in Allison by asking her questions throughout the day and was not solely swayed by her make-over. Either way, the four are all from different social groups but learned about one another and started to see one another differently. That it remains ambiguous whether their relationships will continue points to the enduring conflicts the teen film as a genre addresses. The teens might learn what is right and know what they want, but enacting and living by their personal moral code is difficult to apply in their real world.

Whether they will be true to themselves and retain their new alliances is about withstanding pressure from both authority figures and from peers; it is also related to overcoming the internal pressure teens feel. This leads to the third main binary in *The Breakfast Club*, that between youth and their inner selves, which is uncovered by considering the oppositions between weak/strong, normal/different, and one of the key binary oppositions in the teen film at large, insecurity/confidence. The three forms of pressure teens face – from authority, peers, and themselves – are all intertwined, but it is overcoming the inner struggle that most determines the coming-of-age process.

On the surface, the opposition between weak/strong can be about physical strength and who has the might to stand up to bullies. Indeed, Bender has a domineering physical presence, but the battle of physical strength is quickly tested and dismissed when Andy beats Bender in a wrestling match and then Bender pulls out a knife, which, instead of escalating danger, Allison steals and takes out of play. For the five in detention, the proof of prowess will not be determined by brute force – Andy, who himself was a bully who inflicted bodily harm on someone weaker, could defend himself and others if necessary. Instead, the conflict between weak/strong is more about internal power, about character and fortitude. Whether the teens move from a position of weakness to one of strength has to do with whether they stand up for themselves and for others in the face of threats. Although Bender is the instigator the entire day, and Andy stands up to him early on, telling him to stop berating Claire and Brian, it is Bender who shows his mettle when he sacrifices himself after they get stuck in the hallways, telling the others to go back to the library so they do not get caught (see Figure 2.2). This internal strength also refers to whether Andy, Claire, and Bender will acknowledge Brian and Allison in the face of their friends' likely taunts and whether the romantic couples will survive under the same constraints. Additionally, it has to do with whether all five of them can stand up to their parents and to other authority figures. It is not just strength that will determine the outcome, though.

Having the fortitude of character and the resolve to withstand the conditions of external pressure is closely related to the opposition between insecurity/confidence. The five start the film doubting themselves, keeping

Figure 2.2 Blocked from getting back to the library, Bender decides to take the fall, and the future couples exchange romantic glances.

one another at a distance, either feeling vulnerable or feeling like they have to put up a front in order to impress people, and believe that they are not in control of their own lives. Slowly, however, and with provocations and the help of drugs, they stop hiding and expose their foibles. This comes in similar forms for all of them as they admit to themselves and reveal to one another the truths about themselves, how they feel, what their fears are, and the pressures they face. For Claire, it means being honest when she tells Brian they probably would not be friends because of how important her friends' opinions are to her and how much she hates the coercive conformity; for Bender, it means talking about his abusive father and admitting he too cares what others think because he might do the same thing to Brian as Claire would; for Allison, it is about speaking at all, talking about her home life, and even though it is a highly problematic, cliché makeover, it is also when she shows her face; for Andy, it is telling how much his father berates him and his friends goad him but also about how guilty, remorseful, and empathetic he feels about what he did; and for Brian, it is the intense pressure to get good grades that is so severe he was contemplating suicide after failing an assignment, a burden heavier than the others ever would have imagined. For all five, being brave enough to be honest and come out of hiding shows their increasing strength and confidence. Especially at the group therapy session at the end, 'all five finally give up their false IDs' (Honeycutt 2015: 87), and their armor comes down, showing how they all feel lonely, confused, misunderstood, odd, fake, and under tremendous pressure, even if they think they are the only ones who feel this way.

Their burgeoning confidence is also evident in their acts of rebellion – the two couples that form across social groups, Bender's fist pump of triumph even though he is going to be back in detention for months, and Brian writing a brazen essay. How they arrive at this place of rebellion and confidence stems from acknowledging who they really are, then sharing that identity, and realizing they actually are not alone in how difficult their lives are. In this way, the insecurity/confidence and weak/strong binaries are thus closely related to the opposition between normal/different. Specifically, normalcy or difference is not about conformity but rather relates to how much the teens feel like or akin to others versus how much they feel strange or divergent. Similarly to the inside/outside opposition, there is not one side that is better than the other or that signifies a progression. However, what is more relevant with feeling like an insider or an outsider is social groupings, whereas feeling normal or different has to do with how they see themselves, how they think they compare in relation to others. They all want to feel like they are part of a group, but they also want to be individuals, want to be seen for who they really are, and want to know that who they are is OK.

The way the five come to realize that they are all similar, and that they are normal for feeling different from others, is through the courage to reveal their true selves. The five start the day thinking that all the others fit into a stereotype, that the others could be easily dismissed because of surface appearances. But what they each also think is that as individuals, they are the only ones who know how hard it is to be a teenager in their specific position. What they come to realize is that on the inside, they all have fears and insecurities, they all have problems with their families and their friends, and none of them has it easy or all figured out, even if it seems as though they do. Writing about the 'John Hughes Touch,' *New York Times* critic A. O. Scott identifies this idea of feeling alone in difference and how Hughes's films demonstrate how common that feeling actually is:

> The paradox is that most people feel, and want to be, different. Not to smash the system or flee its clutches, but rather to find a place within it where they can be themselves . . . The great, paradoxical insight of 'The Breakfast Club' is that alienation is the norm, that nerds, jocks, stoners, popular girls and weirdos are all, in their own ways, outsiders.
>
> (2009)

Realizing others are similar to themselves because of how different they are makes them feel not just understood and visible but also more normal and less isolated.

The power of Brian's essay response to Vernon's prompt asking them to write who they think they are, an assignment they ignore writing yet spend the whole day exploring, is multifaceted. It indicates Brian's rebellion against the confines of rigorous academic performance, as well as the influence Claire still holds over him with her blatant manipulation to get him to write the essay, but it also shows his keen wit in understanding the main messages of the film: they are all the same, and they are all different, and it does not matter what people who do not care to really see them think – they know there is more to each of them than it seems. They start to learn that they can accept themselves for who they are because they see bits of themselves in one another, they can relate to one another and not feel so alone. Acceptance from others is still important to them; they know they do not exist in their families or in high school in a vacuum, pointing to a fundamental feature of the genre – teens need to discover their individuality while learning how to integrate into their societies. But they have started along the path of moving away from insecurity and toward confidence, to being closer to understanding who they want to be. Indeed, as a quintessential, canonical teen film that underscores the foundational workings of the genre, *The Breakfast Club* shows on a number of levels how learning to overcome both external and internal conflicts is an essential part of the coming-of-age process as a search for identity.

Genre evolution: reflections of teen life and teen films

Films featuring teen characters in primary roles have been a mainstay in Hollywood for decades. However, it was in the 1980s that these films started to form a more unified genre, that the semantic and syntactic rules became more fully codified, and that the structural elements became more discernable. It was also during this decade that they became a prolific production trend while still harkening back to films made in years prior, indicating that they were relevant to contemporary audiences while addressing enduring societal and cultural concerns. The teen film came to be understood, through repeated textual elements across a variety of different subgenres, as a genre that deals with the way teens discover who they are in the face of both extraordinary and everyday challenges. Of course, even throughout the same decade, the genre contained many types of films, including ones as disparate as *Risky Business*, *A Nightmare on Elm Street* (Craven 1984), *Back to the Future*, *Dirty Dancing*, *The Karate Kid* (Avildsen 1984), and *Young Guns*, each with their own unique features, and one film cannot be seen to encompass all the rest. However, what *The Breakfast Club* does do is exemplify many of the main elements and operating rules, such as the recurring character types and the conflicts between them, that highlight the tropes of the genre.

Labeling *The Breakfast Club* a canonical teen film, especially during its release in the middle of the decade, demonstrates that the genre was reaching a point of maturity. According to life cycle theories proposed by Altman (1999), Cawelti (1979), and Schatz (1981), early in the development of a genre, as a group of similar films are just coalescing into a coherent whole, its rules are still being written. Generally, although not always in chronological order, it is in later stages when those rules become codified. Then when they become so familiar, in order for the form to keep its relevance, films show awareness of the rules, stating them perceptibly, playing with them, and then eventually, modifying them. Reflexivity, then, or the self-awareness of the films as teen film texts, and calling attention to the way the films operate as part of the genre, are indications of this evolutionary process.

Three films in the 1980s illustrate this developing maturity of the form. *Fast Times at Ridgemont High* has teens in the film identifying different character types and their social groups. *The Breakfast Club* does the same but then deconstructs the labels by showing individuals are behind the stereotypes. *Heathers* goes a step further to show a hyper-awareness of the false, constructed nature of those identities. Both *The Breakfast Club* and *Heathers* do not go as far in their reflexivity as parodies like *Scream* (Craven 1996) and *Not Another Teen Movie* (Gallen 2001), films released during the resurgence of the genre a few years later. Instead, the self-aware films in the 1980s focus primarily on the character types that populate high schools and on teen films, not as much on the operating principles of the genre. However, the level of reflexivity that is on display in *The Breakfast Club* is an important signpost in the development of the form and is another reason the film is seen as so archetypical.

Specifically, *The Breakfast Club* focuses its observations on constructed characters, on an almost anthropological examination of social groupings, and on questioning the relevance, accuracy, and effects of labeling people. The film acknowledges that teens get pigeonholed by peers and adults and, to some extent, by themselves. Although they might not be completely accurate representations of teenagers, the characters are nonetheless representative and relatable to classic teen types in previous films and to teens in real life. In this way, the stereotypes are concretized into credible characters. The parts the actors play follow expected patterns: the teens look and act like their types as nerds, jocks, popular girls, rebels, and outcasts, and they act out their assigned roles as typical teens when they oppose adversarial authority figures. But instead of solely following rules, the teens break through the stereotypes and realize their individuality. As they do so, the film calls attention to the artifice and harm of those standard conventions. What remains a question, though, is the extent of how aware the teens, or the filmmakers, are of the authenticity of their characters. There is actually some validity to the roles and labels the teens inhabit, and the identities and social groupings are based on elements of the reality of teen life, even if they are constructed. Feeling pressure to conform might mean the teens are pretending, but those performances affect who they are. Yes, there is more to people than their labels, but as they simultaneously try to live up to their status and break free from their confines, those labels play a part in shaping character.

When looking at the reflexivity of *The Breakfast Club*, then, it becomes apparent that the film is more aware of and more interested in commenting on teen life than teen films. It calls attention to the artificiality inherent in teen labels and teen socialization processes. At the same time, it does so with earnestness as it addresses the significant impact of those roles and relationships and how important it is to recognize them as constructs in order to break through them. Essentially, the stereotypes are effectively built up in order to be meaningfully torn down. This level of awareness is a necessary step in the evolution of the genre – by codifying the rules, the iconic character types are established and tied to reality, and then they are refuted in order to be fully understood. As such, *The Breakfast Club* exists in a moment of maturity of the form; it refines the rules of the genre and addresses the issues with sincerity. Although the film is not as interested in genre reflexivity as are satires, parodies, or spoofs, its awareness of the teen film as representative of contemporary teen life is unmistakable.

In an ironic and problematic twist, the actors who starred in *The Breakfast Club* suffered similar trials to the characters they portrayed. The Brat Pack label was coined a few months after the film was released by a reporter doing an exposé on young stars in Hollywood, capturing just a sliver of the lives of a select few of them. But the catchy label stuck, the actors stopped being seen as individuals with talent and burgeoning careers, and instead were grouped together and typecast. As quick as people were to grasp the important messages of *The Breakfast Club*, they were just as quick to dismiss its lessons. In a way, this building up and then breaking down of stereotypes in the film, and then reinstating them for the stars of the film afterward, corresponds to a possible trajectory of what happens to the teens on Monday, even though it is not what we hope. While the Brat Pack affiliation ultimately became a calling card that bolstered the actors' lasting fame and kept continuing attention on their films, it took years to see past the label. Life that was imitated in art became reflected in reality, cementing the status of *The Breakfast Club* as a quintessential teen film and the genre as one that addresses how we find out who we are and how we live our lives.

3 Teen problems in the 1980s, and Generation X and baby boomers just don't get along

Films are cultural products that reveal information about the time and place in which they are made. As artifacts, they contain ideology, or elements of the values, beliefs, and ideals of contemporary culture. Narrative and formal analyses, specifically those confined to the bounds of the text, are valuable for showing the inner workings of the film and explain how the genre functions. A cultural studies approach, though, which examines the film and the context of its production, performs textual analysis while taking into account the specific historical moment in which the film was made, and considers issues related to representations of various groups, as well as to political, economic, and societal concerns. Robert Stam points out that 'texts are embedded in a social matrix' (2000: 225), and Lois Tyson notes that they always have an 'ideological "story" to tell' (2015: 283), indicating the interrelationship between films, genres, and culture and the importance of contextualizing their analyses in this manner. Indeed, the depiction of youth and their coming-of-age process in *The Breakfast Club* is determined by the film's historical context.

Moreover, saying that films contain ideological representations of the time in which they are produced is especially noteworthy when dealing with teen films. As Joe Austin and Michael Willard point out in their introduction to *Generations of Youth*,

> the public debates surrounding 'youth' are important forums where new understandings about the past, present, and future of public life are encoded, articulated, and contested. 'Youth' becomes a metaphor for perceived social change and its projected consequences, and as such it is an enduring locus for displaced social anxieties.
>
> (1998: 1)

Teen films on their own contain these larger cultural concerns, but when thinking of *The Breakfast Club*, there is additional meaning – the film often comes out on top of retrospective lists that label it a model specimen of the genre and of the 1980s (Rettenmund 1996; 'Readers' Poll' 2014; Entertainment Weekly Staff 2015). Implied with this status is that the film is rife with symbolism and signification.

While *The Breakfast Club* is arguably exemplary, its lofty classification does not mean it stands in for the entire genre, the decade, or youth more broadly. Even though its structural elements are the same as others in the genre, it is a specific type of teen film that focuses on rebellion and one that was released in the midst of a production surge of a wide variety of teen films. Additionally, while the 1980s are often called 'the eighties,' a term that marks cohesion of calendar years as well as common sentiments and attitudes, there are complex issues that arise when trying to periodize a decade according to accepted generalizations. An era, when examined more closely, is always full of heterogeneity, contradictions, and tension. And even if identifying the 1980s as remarkably consistent, ideologies within a culture are never monolithic. As Robin Wood illustrates in 'Ideology, Genre, Auteur' (2012 (1977): 80), a culture's beliefs are incongruous and contain numerous unresolvable tensions. Furthermore, even saying that a film presents typical teens is problematic too. In Catherine Driscoll's study of the genre, she asks whether the 'teen film actually represent[s] teenagers at all' (2011: 5), especially when taking into account the ages of the people involved in film production and the limited slice of life presented.

With the challenges of labeling *The Breakfast Club* a representative sample of one duly noted, a cultural studies analysis is nonetheless edifying for revealing issues related to representation, historical forces, and generational conflict. Specifically, this chapter proceeds first by looking at select political, economic, and social changes the country was facing in parallel with the ways different groups were affected by these changes, and at the ways these concerns were manifest in the film. *The Breakfast Club* shows challenges teens face stemming from shifting cultural norms relating to class differences, increasing divorce rates, and abuse, while it ignores others related to race and foreign policy. Certain complex problems arise, for example, including issues dealing with socioeconomic status and women's sexuality. However, some predicaments are given pat solutions, such as when the two romantic couples form, while other dilemmas are left hanging, such as how the teens will face continuing pressure from their parents and peers.

The next section of the chapter addresses the conflict between youth and adults in the context of generational discourse. Essential to the story and to its time of production in the 1980s is the conflict between generations, specifically, the baby boomers and Generation X. The boomers, the generation that came of age in the 1960s and 1970s, redefined the way youth came to be seen as an attitude instead of an age. As a result, the boomers kept up what are often considered youthful and selfish attitudes about putting themselves first even as they grew into the roles of parents and authority figures. They did so, however, as the next generation, which had at the time not yet been given a name, felt like they had to take on adult roles while having no role models to show them how to navigate these responsibilities. *The Breakfast Club* pits teens and adults against each other, to a somewhat exaggerated extent, but does so in order to show the primacy of the peer group during the particularly fraught period of adolescent development. In so doing, it also highlights the effects of contemporary attitudes about generational norms.

A cultural studies approach examines a text in its historical context and looks at dominant ideologies, as well as the challenges to those ideologies, that are depicted in the film. Importantly, this analytical framework also focuses on ways often marginalized groups are represented or made invisible and takes into account generational discourses surrounding youth and adults that are prominently displayed. Even in a popular teen film with troubling gender politics and a lack of diversity, there are revealing moments of subversion where the dominant is contested. And while the film was not produced by Generation X teenagers (although its young cast did have creative input), its success and lasting resonance speaks to both its contemporary and continued relevance. Analyzing *The Breakfast Club* in its cultural and historical context adds to an understanding of the lived experience of adolescents in the 1980s and further explains why the film remains so canonical.

Representation

Politically, the 1980s were marked by an escalation of the Cold War and a return to conservatism after the more liberal 1960s and 1970s. Instead of the civil rights and women's rights movements that seemed to dominate the previous period, there were backlashes against more progressive values (Faludi 1991). These widespread attitudes coincided with an economic recession in the beginning of the decade, rapidly increasing prosperity in the mid-1980s, and growing interest in the pursuit of wealth as the decade progressed. But only certain sectors of the population reaped the benefits of the booming economy before the stock market crashed in 1987. Meanwhile, socioeconomic group disparities were intensifying as the poor got poorer, social programs were cut, and the drug and AIDS crises hit. The country was facing vast systemic problems, but the solutions, in line with American ideology, lay in individuals being able to overcome difficulties and succeed on their own, not in policy changes. The cliché expression, then and now, is that you should 'pull yourself up by your bootstraps' and improve a situation on your own.

The escalation and eventual end of the Cold War was in the forefront of the political arena. Diversity was on the rise; the 1990 US census reported that over one-third of those aged 10 to 29 were nonwhite or Hispanic (quoted in Owen 1997: 2). These issues, however, are glaringly absent from the very sheltered, very white *Breakfast Club*. Although these absences are certainly notable, how problematic they are is debatable. An article in *The Independent* discussing the quintessential nature of the film notes that outside

> the school gates, a cold war was raging, Africa was starving and crack cocaine and Aids [sic] had begun to wreak havoc in US cities. Hughes didn't take any notice of that. The director understood that most teenagers are preoccupied with their self-image and how others see them.
>
> (Manzoor 2004)

Of course, these issues and their nonappearance are of concern, but their lack is circumscribed by a text that pays attention to teens whose focus is on the self within their own insulated communities. While this self-focused nature of the teens can be read as indicative of privilege, the film is also important for bringing to light that just because a certain racial or socioeconomic group appears on the surface to have it easy does not mean that they do not also have serious problems.

While the film does not address cultural studies issues of race, nationality, and disability, it does tackle concerns about class, gender, and sexuality (although not sexual orientation directly). Not surprisingly, the film's positions regarding these matters closely parallel Hughes's biography and reported personal politics: Hughes, who was a baby boomer, was actually a conservative Republican and was more an anti-authoritarian than liberal member of the counterculture (Honeycutt 2015: 7; Weiss 2006). The personal political issues that seemed to affect him most were those having to do with class consciousness; he was aware of the ways income disparities affected social status because of having grown up working class in affluent suburbs (Honeycutt 2015: 25), and his films specifically focused on how socioeconomic status forms the basis for teen social cliques (Bleach 2010: 25). Hughes was not alone in these concerns. The 1980s are often seen as a time marked by materialism, and indeed 'yuppies,' the nickname for young urban professionals dedicated to the relentless pursuit of wealth, are associated with the decade as a symbol of consumerism and greed. As Jane Feuer describes in *Seeing Through the Eighties*, though, yuppies were actually members of the 'formerly rebellious' baby boomers (1995: 14). Boomers, because of their population size and influence, were still setting the cultural tone of the time, with the focus on money permeating through generations. Class, according to Hughes, was 'not something you skipped but were defined by' (Weiss 2006).

Signs of class difference are apparent in *The Breakfast Club* (as well as throughout Hughes's oeuvre). From the first moment the characters are introduced and throughout the day, their class statuses are revealed by the clothing they wear, the cars their parents drive, and even the food they eat. Claire's wealth is the most obvious because of the prominent framing of her father's BMW car logo, her designer clothes, and her sushi lunch. As a testament to the way teens mimic broader attitudes about affluence, she even asks why she has to serve detention because she does not think her 'crime' of skipping school to go shopping merits such punishment, and if she must, why she has to serve it in the same room as the others, questioning their sameness and why the rules still apply to someone as privileged as she is. Meanwhile, Andy and Brian's working class status is revealed by the cars their parents drive, a Ford Bronco for Andy and a Dodge for Brian, and by the standard sandwiches and thermos packed for lunch. But the conversations with their parents are more telling – both sets of parents are worried that their sons are endangering their futures by messing up in school; the parents know they do not have the financial resources to support them if they do not get ahead by their own athletic or scholarly abilities. Bender meanwhile, walks to school, brings no food with him, and tells of his abuse and likely poverty by the home life he reenacts for the others, specifically the cigar burns on his arm and the cigarettes given as gifts. His behavior problems could be the result of personality and parenting, but could also be because of hunger and lack of resources.

Interestingly, Allison's status is indicative of the ways both background and character contribute to students' standing in school. While not as obvious as Claire's material displays of wealth, Allison gets dropped off in a new Cadillac. At times during the day, she talks of sessions with a psychiatrist and places she may have visited. While it is not clear how much of what Allison says is true or how much her parents might pay for her therapy and travels, her parents' luxury car and the way they ignore her speaks to a home life similar to Cameron's in Hughes's *Ferris Bueller's Day Off*, one with money but devoid of affection. As a result, she is not well-adjusted and is on the outside of the school's social circles. Claire's affluence, meanwhile, is apparent and raises doubts about how much her parents' wealth contributes to her popularity, specifically how much her friends like her for who she is or for what she has. While social status is not granted by money alone, class division as a primary source of rivalries is evident across Hughes's films – Bender taunts Claire, calling her a 'richie,' a term that would later be used in *Pretty in Pink* to describe the wealthy and popular kids in school who look down on everyone else. Echoing socioeconomic tensions in the country at large, high school hostilities show how the increasing divisions between those with money and those without affect interpersonal relationships and contribute to a lack of understanding between classes.

The pressures and problems the teens face to succeed inside and beyond high school know no class boundaries, but the burden of facing challenges relating to sex and gender fall more squarely on the young women in the film. Andy and Bender do still perform masculinity, demonstrating their athleticism and 'tough guy' acts of rebellion, and show how even 'rebellion can itself be cast as a norm of youthful masculinity' (Smith 2017: 5). Andy recollects his father's taunts when he tells of targeting Larry Lester because he was 'skinny and weak,' qualities winners are not supposed to embody, and Bender has the derogatory slur 'fag' written across his locker, both acts they think reinforce their powerful, heterosexual male standing. Even when Brian, who is not as physically dominant, is asked early on whether he has had sex, the conversation is quickly dismissed as something amusing, as a rite of passage that a 'nerd' or 'geek' of course has not had yet. However, the males are for the most part not the ones judged based on gender norms or sexual experience. As an example, Andy and Bender are never even asked about their virginity.

Hughes's films are notable for having strong female protagonists, for female characters who are individuals unto themselves instead of there to further the male character's development (Freeman 2016: 68). However, his portrayal of young women also reinforces traditional and neo-conservative gender stereotypes (De Vaney 2002; Roberts 2016). Claire is berated and tormented the entire day for being a 'princess,' for being a spoiled rich girl who has her father wrapped around her finger and who gets almost everything she wants. Bender's attacks against her are particularly vicious; he calls her names, makes her cry, and at one point, sticks his face between her legs when he is hiding under her desk. In a retrospective article in light of the #MeToo movement that saw women becoming more empowered to come out against their harassers in the late-2010s, Ringwald (2018) stated that she was particularly disturbed when she saw this scene again because she did not realize the inference was that Bender likely physically assaulted Claire at that moment. And yet, when the film was released in the mid-1980s, their coupling was seen as a triumphant culmination of a plot line. Not only do Claire and Bender end up romantically linked, but in order for their coupling to even happen, Claire had to seek out Bender in the closet and make the first move. The message is that his abusive behavior is not only tolerated, it is romanticized. Indicating that the reason he was so cruel to her was because he secretly liked her, and that she understood his feelings and intentions, reinforces violent and aggressive behavior.

Although Bender is the main instigator, Allison and the others also confront Claire, trying to get her to admit the extent of her sexual experiences. Granted, Allison is under no obligation to ally herself with Claire just because they are both women, but she also displays the unchecked sexism in the film when instead of defending Claire against the attacks about her sex status, she is pitted against her, calling her a 'tease' and cajoling her into revealing more than she wanted to by pretending to be a nymphomaniac. Allison, however, is particularly astute, understanding and vocalizing the politicized 'double-edged sword' of female sexuality when she states that 'if you say you haven't, you're a prude. If you say you have, you're a slut. It's a trap. You want to, but you can't, and when you do, you wish you didn't.' She was not just identifying a Madonna-whore complex, because in this case, neither position is desirable. By these measures, women, and especially young women, are left with few good options.

Notably, that the teens are even talking so freely about having sex speaks to changing social mores. In the 1980s, reports on sexual behavior and attitudes revealed that people were starting to have sex at younger ages (Tropiano 2006: 149). If in previous eras societal constraints stressed that teens should remain chaste, after the sexual revolution of the 1960s and 1970s, teen sex was more commonplace and there was pressure to be sexually active. However, these changing beliefs and practices do not mean there were not still stigmas around sex – there were, especially for women. Women being able to have sex more freely went along with increased women's rights and more equality, things seen as threats to traditional patriarchy. Instead of having the freedom that came with making decisions about their own bodies came double standards and fears of damaged reputations or 'slut shaming.' Meanwhile men were revered for their experience and were called 'studs' instead of 'sluts' if they had sex.

Although Allison states incisive observations about female sexuality, it is her and Claire's interactions after the big reveals of the group therapy session that expose the film's problematic conformity to traditional stereotypes and gendered double standards. For a film that espouses self-acceptance and seeing others for who they are, Allison's makeover hardly seems to fit. With Claire's assistance, Allison supposedly becomes more attractive, and Andy is so taken with her that the budding feelings he had can now fully blossom. As a narrative device, a big reveal works, and the makeover's saving grace is that instead of putting more makeup on, Allison's face is made visible when her original dark makeup is taken off and her hair is pulled back (see Figure 3.1). In retrospect, however, even Sheedy, who convinced Hughes to tone down the scene by having makeup come off instead of added on, commented she thinks that 'we probably should have left her alone or tried something a little less drastic and more original' (2007: xii). That a

Figure 3.1 Allison's makeover reveals her face but remains a cliché.

woman must change physically to be noticed and desired further reinforces the belief that women's importance and worth lies in appearances instead of character.

The Breakfast Club is a film of its time and of its director. It actually calls attention to issues of class and gender that were so pressing in the 1980s; however, it also further reinforces some troubling stereotypes at the same time it is so interested in disavowing others. Perhaps in a testament to the way it at least tries to address class and gender inequities but acknowledges its shortcomings, the film ends with Claire giving Bender a single diamond earing (see Figure 3.2). Unlike in *Some Kind of Wonderful*, where Keith deliberates throughout on spending his college tuition on a pair of diamond earrings for the girl he loves, this gesture is tacked on at the end. It is not clear why Claire gives Bender the earring: does she want to assert her independence, and does he want to show off to his friends? Does it emphasize class inequality and rebellion? Is it switching gender roles so the girl is giving the boy the equivalent of a pin while simultaneously encouraging his misogyny? Do they really like each other, and will this be the token object that ties them together? The confusion and uncertainty of this both classed and gendered exchange speaks to a film trying to advance the idea that teenagers, and those giving them a platform to speak, are aware of the complexity of their time but still do not have it all figured out.

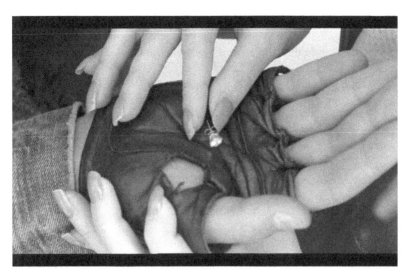

Figure 3.2 Claire gives Bender her diamond earring; her freshly manicured nails contrast with his torn leather gloves.

Generations

The way the abundant upheavals around political, economic, social, and technological issues affected teens were also felt in the conflicts between and discourse around the two successive generations that were in the spotlight during the decade. Generation X, or those born roughly from the early 1960s to the late 1970s, did not get a recognized name until the 1990s when Douglas Coupland's novel about three underemployed youths living in California, *Generation X: Tales for an Accelerated Culture* (1991), was released. Even without an official label, though, they were the generation coming of age during the 1980s, those who were experiencing extreme class disparities and changing family dynamics, all while being criticized for being disaffected and disillusioned. Meanwhile, the baby boomers, those born between the mid-1940s to the early 1960s, were given the name because of the birth rate surge post-World War II, and were labeled as an idealist and iconoclastic generation who were supposedly going to change the world for the better.

That there would be clashes between the two generations was inevitable considering their differing traits but also because of the way youth was being defined and redefined in US culture. Even though there has always been tension between parents and children as part of the coming-of-age process, the concept of adolescence, of a distinct period between childhood and adulthood, was not introduced until the early 1900s. As the US started to experience more prosperity, teens did not immediately start work and instead continued their education. This growing wealth, extended leisure time, and especially starting in the 1950s, increased targeted marketing toward demographic groups meant that teens were seen as a separate cohort. Often, these changes played out in the teen film, the genre that represents the coming-of-age process of its youthful protagonists, as conflict between teens and their elders. Even if the parents were two generations removed, depending, for example, if the parents and children were born in the early part or tail end of their respective generations, the conflict between two consecutive generations was the one often depicted on screen. Ever since James Dean's anguish in *Rebel Without a Cause*, and his utter disappointment in his parents for their inability to be proper role models, teens in teen films have frequently been depicted as being at odds with authority figures.

The specific reasons for these conflicts, however, have changed over time because not only are the clashes between the younger and older generations, but they are also between different generation groups. In Strauss and Howe's (1991) analysis of generations in the United States, they show that while we tend to associate some attributes with children, youth, adults, and seniors, each generation group (such as baby boomers and Generation X) has distinct attributes, meaning that the attributes associated with each age range are different depending on the generational group identity. So, while the boomers are associated with idealism in youth, Generation X is associated with cynicism; even if youth in general is correlated with rebellion, it takes different forms. Because the boomers were such a large group and one of the first young cohorts to be delineated via widespread marketing campaigns, they began to redefine the qualities expected of youth as an age group. When Generation X attitudes were perceived as different, as not following expected suit because of not conforming to boomer-typical notions of youthful idealism and hopefulness, they were criticized. Allison's acts of defiance in *The Breakfast Club* are a case in point: instead of political marches, her protests against the status quo take the form of alienation and pessimism, as well as boredom – the reason she is in detention is because she had nothing better to do. Being disaffected and full of angst was an overarching ethos of Generation X in the 1980s and would evolve into Generation X being associated with apathy and slackers in the 1990s. Except instead of a function of generational identity, even other generational cohorts at the time were feeling cynical because of the distressing era in which they were all living (O'Toole 1998). Regardless of the similar affects though, the effect was that the gap and lack of understanding between the two groups grew.

While generations are often defined by people who share a kinship, are born between specific date ranges (the beginnings and endings of which are not precise), and have shared experiences of significant events, often with those occurring during adolescence having the most impact, of course, no one generation is homogenous and not all its members are the same (Mannheim 1952: 304–312; Schuman and Rogers 2004: 250; Dimock 2018). Just like with the terms and concepts of 'ideology,' 'the US,' and the 'eighties,' though, certain generalizations and discourses around labels are useful to show how a generation is broadly understood, especially during the same historical time period. For general traits emblematic of the baby boomers, aside from shifting away from activism and toward consumerism and neoconservatism as they grew older in the 1980s, they were also associated with redefining the idea of 'youth' as a personality trait instead of an age. Age ranges for when adolescence begins and ends are somewhat more precise, delimited by biological functions around puberty. However, for the term 'youth,' often the end is vague because markers of adulthood, such as starting careers, getting married, having children, buying a house, etc., are variable. But these changes were more pronounced as the boomers entered adulthood. As Lawrence Grossberg describes in 'Is There Rock after Punk?' boomers redefined 'youth as an attitude' but with troubling consequences: because they were not maturing into their roles as adults, members of the next generation compensated by being 'increasingly troubled and adult-like' (1986: 64). Teens in the 1980s felt like there was no one to look up to, and that they had to take care of things on their own with no assurances for the future.

If in the 1980s the concept of youth was undergoing an identity crisis, actual youth were in actual crisis. Strauss and Howe (1991) describe a number of features associated with the generation coming of age during the decade, many that were on display in *The Breakfast Club*. Generation X faced dire economic prospects and broke a long-standing historical trend when they were not expected to do better financially than their parents. There were also ever-widening gaps between rich and poor. These economic concerns are evident in the pressure Andy's and Brian's parents put on them to succeed, while the class disparities are visible with Bender's poverty and the animosity he felt toward Claire because of her wealth.

Family life was also very different for Generation X. Divorce rates were rapidly climbing, with teens feeling like previous generations were 'worth' parents staying together while they were not; Claire's discussion of her parents' troubled marriage illustrates the increasingly common trend. Additionally, more mothers had to work outside the home to keep up with rising costs of living expenses, and because of growing dissatisfaction with domesticity and its concomitant lack of financial independence. This meant that there were more 'latchkey kids' – youths who would come home after school to no adult supervision and who, by necessity, were becoming more self-reliant (Blakemore 2015). One of the common afterschool activities that occupied the unsupervised time was watching television – in addition to being called the 'Latchkey Generation,' they were also called the 'MTV Generation' because of the introduction of cable television and the popularity of the music channel during the decade. While the name is an indication of technological change, it also has to do with the idea that TV acted as a babysitter. That there is an extended music video-type sequence in *The Breakfast Club* where the teens dance around the library points to the influence of MTV at the time.

Instead of the 'Latchkey' or 'MTV' generation, a generation of kids left to take care of themselves, the boomers were alternatively called the 'Me Generation,' referring to self-improvement tendencies and self-involved attitudes they were associated with during Generation X's adolescence. As a result, larger societal values shifted to placing attention on adults versus on children. Adults, then, were watching out for themselves, while teens were left to navigate adult responsibilities on their own. Seen in light of generational discourse, Vernon and Carl's conversation in the basement takes on new meaning (see Figure 3.3). When Vernon states that he is worried about who will take care of him, instead of viewing it as a shared fear between him and the teens upstairs, it is more self-centered; as an adult responsible for students, his main concern is his welfare, not theirs. This selfish

Figure 3.3 Vernon shares beers and fears with Carl in the basement.

attitude, combined with Vernon's moral corruption, bungling authoritative-ness, and the overall lack of trust between youth and adults, is indicative of oppositional stances that represent cultural differences between successive generations.

The distance was felt in the criticisms each lobbed toward the other and the lack of empathy and sympathy between the generations. The problems that ensued from these disappointments were internalized by the teens and articulated in their group dynamics. Children felt like they could not look up to their parents, students felt like they could not trust their teachers. With ineffective, and even detrimental, authority figures, teens were left to be independent – they had to rely on themselves and their peers to solve prob-lems on their own. One of the most severe ways these generational attributes was articulated in *The Breakfast Club* is with Brian's suicide attempt. He feels so much pressure to conform to his parents' standards and to achieve academic success that when his grade point average is jeopardized by an F, fearing that his life is ruined, he is driven to contemplate suicide (see Fig-ure 3.4). The flare gun he brought to school went off in his locker before he could attempt hurting himself, so rather than adults showing concern and wondering why a good student without any previous behavior problems would do such a thing, they rushed to punish him by sending him to deten-tion. Most likely, he never told anyone else of his suicidal thoughts; if he had, the fact that he was put in detention would be even more disturbing. Instead of disclosing his intent to any adults, he only reveals the truth to the

Figure 3.4 The pressure Brian feels is almost life-threatening.

rest of the group. What the teens discover is that in the face of authority fig-ures who do not understand or support them, they must rely on themselves and their peers to get through the difficult period of adolescence.

Instead of youth needing to be indoctrinated into the societal structures and norms dictated by the previous generations, *The Breakfast Club* shows how teens try to forge their own paths. None of them wants to be like their parents; they do not want to use, abuse, or ignore their own children and instead want to remember what it was like to be young, want to be able to understand the issues the next generation will face. Although it is easy to fall into the logic of the film that authority figures are the source of all ills, it is important to remember that essential to the coming-of-age process is youth taking responsibility for their own actions and seizing control over the types of adults they will become. In the context of discerning how ideological values are enunciated in texts, analyzing the representation of generations in the film is not a way to lay blame; rather, it is to demonstrate how *The Break-fast Club* adds to our understanding of the genre and to the contemporary culture that produced it and other films. Instead of pointing fingers to one source where the problems originate, what teen films of the 1980s show, and what a cultural studies analysis of *The Breakfast Club* exemplifies, is that the problems are multiple. But while the fundamental nature of the conflict between youth and authority endures, the film emphasizes the imperative teens have to solve problems on their own, regardless of whether or not they have any guidance from adults on their journey. Even though most heroes in stories must overcome obstacles and succeed by themselves or with a trusted group of allies, that the heroes saddled with these responsibilities in teen films are still adolescents speaks to disconcerting cultural standards for youth and adults.

In different ways, all the teens in *The Breakfast Club* are crying for atten-tion; are confused, angry, and scared; feel pressure to perform and conform; and are afraid of the consequences if they do not. While they rebel by cutting school, causing mischief, or being harmful, their ultimate act of rebellion lies in realizing self-knowledge and reaching self-acceptance. By revealing themselves to one another, even in the face of parental, peer, and internal pressure, and by sharing the experience of living through detention, high school, their families, adolescence, and the decade, they achieve a sense of camaraderie, further reinforcing the kinship between members of Genera-tion X. These generationally defined paths to self-actualization became part of the teen socialization process during the decade. Arguably, because the teen film as a genre was becoming codified at the same time and because each film in a genre is symbolic of the larger mythical issues upon which the narratives are based, the coming-of-age processes that are so clearly and cogently encapsulated in *The Breakfast Club* become some of the tropes most closely associated and recognized with teen films as a whole. Just as the boomers tried to redefine youth, *The Breakfast Club* helped redefine the teen film.

Although the teens are hopeful that they will not make the same mistakes as the generations that came before, they do not know what the future holds. Almost like in the Peter Pan tales, the potential exists that just the act of getting older means that people might forget what it is like to be young. Again, Allison is the one to make the trenchant comment when she states that it is unavoidable, 'when you grow up, your heart dies.' But what is not clear is whether it is just their parents who do not understand, or parents in general who would never understand. Is it a problem with the generation that comes before, or is it the nature of growing older that is the source of the disconnect? Is it a problem with the generation that is currently coming of age, or is it a fundamental aspect of the conflicts between young and old that makes the relationships so fraught? What the teens as adolescents are not aware of is how much their parents or teachers might know because authority figures are never seen outside the teens' perspective. Of course, there are adults who do understand (Hughes was perhaps one), and the teens promise not to be like their parents. But just like the question of whether the five will remain friends on Monday, the question of how youth will turn out as they age is left unanswered too.

4   The synergistic effects of the marketing and the music

Regardless of how good a film may be because of its content and form, how it touches on contemporary cultural issues, or how audiences come to love it while it is in theaters or years later, if a studio does not think a film will sell, it is unlikely that it will get made or released in the first place. Commercialism is *de rigueur* in Hollywood and was especially so in the 1980s. This was a decade that saw threatening declines in box-office attendance at the same time as the importance of ancillary markets like home video and cable was increasing. These new areas relied on successful box-office runs though – if a film did well in theatrical release, it was likely to do better in subsequent release windows also, but if it bombed in the theaters, the ancillary markets often suffered too. Another reason for the increasing significance of making and marketing commercial products was the waves of mergers and acquisitions sweeping through Hollywood at the time. As part of large conglomerates, the studios had to show they were profitable not just as entities unto themselves but also to the companies of which they were now just another holding. Universal, the studio behind *The Breakfast Club* as distributor, was part of MCA/Universal, which in just a few years in 1990 would be bought by Japanese manufacturer Matsushita. And actually both MCA and A&M (one of the production companies behind the film) were record companies first. This is especially notable considering the importance of the music and soundtrack to *The Breakfast Club* and also indicates the significance of the multi-media approaches used to sell films and related products across several parts of the same corporation in the 1980s. As much as *The Breakfast Club* had to offer in terms of content, the film needed to be packaged and sold to both the studio and the audience to prove its worth in the marketplace.

The goals of marketing in the film business are rather straightforward: the intent is to sell the movie and its associated products. The question is usually about how best to do so, especially in a crowded field. There was an abundance of teen films being released around the same time; in the same month *The Breakfast Club* premiered in February 1985, two other teen films hit theaters as well: *Turk 182* (Clark) and *Vision Quest* (Becker). As a result, *The Breakfast Club* would have to rely on the familiarity and recognition that the teen film genre would bring while also setting itself apart as different from the rest of the current offerings. It would carefully time its release and use multi-pronged marketing campaigns to reach its desired audiences. Additionally, it would incorporate music in the film, promote the soundtrack, and use music in advertisements. Indeed, *synergy* was another important buzzword in Hollywood, especially during the 1980s. The idea is that one product – a film – could be sold across multiple arms of a conglomerate, that the branding of the product would help sell movie tickets and also help increase the sales of related products, such as the soundtrack. By positioning the film across the media landscape and by using its specific content to entice audiences in the marketing of the film, *The Breakfast Club* made the most of its generational appeal. This chapter examines the specifics of how the content of the film, the marketing strategies, and the music tie-ins all worked together to position *The Breakfast Club* as an exemplary entry in the corpus of the teen film genre in the 1980s.

Marketing: the content

One of the primary ways a film is identified, and thus sold and recognized, is by its genre designation. Because of their familiarity and their repeated patterns, genres are a shorthand way for audiences to understand what kinds of films they like and want to watch again. Genres establish a horizon of expectations, while specific genre films satisfy those expectations. Or as Schatz notes, film genres are like a contract, and genre films are instances where that contract is honored (1981: 16). The primary expectations that the teen film genre carries are that the films will feature young actors portraying teenage characters and that the films will tell a coming-of-age story. These stories can range in tone and content. The overarching category includes a variety of subgenres and genre hybrids, such as teen comedy and drama, as well as teen romance, action, fantasy, and horror, as examples. Regardless, though, of the specific type of teen film, the genre as a whole is marked by teens who go through this development process questioning their identities, not just as individuals but also as members of a group, and questioning who they are now and who they want to become, while also trying to enjoy themselves, at least a little.

The Breakfast Club fits squarely into these overall definitions of the genre and, indeed, helped to define the genre as it was coalescing over the course of the 1980s. The film features rebellious high school students figuring out who they are and their place in the social hierarchies of both the school and their families. They are at odds with members of the older generation, try to enjoy their youth while also suffering through its hardships, and contemplate both how much the actions that got them in detention matter and how much their time at this particular Saturday detention will mean in the future. In addition, the tone of the film also fits across both drama and comedy, with subplots of romance appearing as well. By containing the quintessential elements of the teen film, a form that was in the midst of being crystalized, *The Breakfast Club* established its place as a genre film and bolstered its appeal to audiences interested in this type of film.

However, it can actually be problematic to rely too much on familiar, and currently fashionable, genres as a selling point. Hollywood is known for being repetitious; when a certain type of film is popular, more and more related films will be made in a similar vein until a little while after that type is no longer successful at the box office or in the ancillary markets. As such, genres often go through cycles. One kind of cycle can relate to the 'life cycle' of how a genre develops, where it moves from the initial stages of codifying its rules to later stages of being more self-reflexive (Schatz 1981; Altman 1999). Here, however, the relevance is that genres can also go through cycles of popularity, times when a group of films of a similar type are made in rapid succession but then fall out of favor (Altman 1999; Klein 2011). The quickly and easily recognizable formula cannot be leaned upon too heavily if the film wants to be seen as something both familiar and different.

Keeping this strategy in mind was especially relevant considering teen films made up approximately 9.5% of all films released in the US in 1984 and almost 12% in 1985 (Nelson 2011: 168). To break from the pack, although *The Breakfast Club* had the typical settings and iconic characters familiar from teen films, it used a combination of dramatic and comedic tones, contained multiple character types all interacting with one another to appeal to various youth audiences, and carefully matched the accompanying music to narrative elements instead of tacking it on as a selling point. In addition, its R-rating was given because of language and content, not because of overt sex scenes or gory horror, some of the most common reasons for the more mature rating. While this may have restricted some younger audiences from seeing the film in the theaters, it also indicated that the film was going to be dealing with serious and complex narrative issues, that it was not meant to be disregarded as a trifle. Instead of audiences feeling like they were being pandered to, they could instead feel like they were being spoken to and spoken for because of the earnest nature of the content.

While the genre designation is one of its most quickly recognizable qualities and selling points, another is its cast of featured actors. Obviously, because there were so many teen films released around the same time period, a number of young actors were required to fill the roles therein. As a result, many of the actors who frequently appeared in the genre films were becoming well known. Actors, and especially famous ones, are sometimes considered 'human capital,' and as Justin Wyatt describes in *High Concept*, stars are 'perhaps the most significant pre-sold property from a commercial standpoint' (1994: 31). Having popular actors play well-defined character types in familiar genre films becomes a shorthand identifier and is a way to quickly and easily market a film. In essence, popular actors in familiar roles can indicate a brand or a label that makes a product immediately understood and therefore easier to sell.

The Breakfast Club featured some of the most famous teen actors of the decade. Stars Emilio Estevez, Anthony Michael Hall, Judd Nelson, Molly Ringwald, and Ally Sheedy would soon become known as and form part of the 'Brat Pack.' According to Blum (1985), who coined the term, the young actors

> make major movies with big directors and get fat contracts and lim-
> ousines. They have top agents and protective P.R. people. They have
> legions of fans who write them letters, buy them drinks, follow them
> home. And, most important, they sell movie tickets. Their films are
> often major hits, and the bigger the hit, the more money they make, and
> the more money they make, the more like stars they become.
>
> (1985: 42)

Interestingly though, while the article increased the star power of the actors in the film, it actually appeared in an issue timed to coincide with the release of *St. Elmo's Fire* (a film which featured three of the same actors) in June 1985, four months after *The Breakfast Club* came out. The 'Brat Pack' term itself did not help the initial box office of *The Breakfast Club* but did help with its subsequent recognizability and lasting fame. Before the article, the actors were starting to earn recognition and even praise; after the article, the actors were unfairly typecast and their talent questioned, but their star power, and thus marketability, increased exponentially nonetheless.

The young actors were the visible face of the film on screen, but behind the scenes, the most notable 'star' was writer and director John Hughes. At the time especially, coming off the success he had as writer of *National Lampoon's Vacation* and *Mr. Mom*, both in 1983, and the popular *Sixteen Candles*, which he wrote and directed the prior year, Hughes was becoming a brand unto himself. In just a short period over the following two years, he would go on to write and direct the teen films *Weird Science* (also with Anthony Michael Hall) and *Ferris Bueller's Day Off*, and write *Pretty in Pink* (also with Molly Ringwald) and *Some Kind of Wonderful*. His close association with the teen film, along with his famous collaboration with Molly Ringwald, led Richard Corliss, in a *Time* magazine feature about the actress in 1986, to point to Hughes's prominent role in Hollywood. Corliss quoted Ned Tanen, producer of *The Breakfast Club* and noted studio head, labeling Hughes the 'Steven Spielberg of youth comedy' (Tanen, quoted in Corliss 1986). In her book about the impact of John Hughes and the Brat Pack, Susannah Gora writes that 'Hughes had become a famous, rich director, one of a handful of Hollywood directors recognizable enough that teenage kids would excitedly come up to him in public' (Gora 2010: 186). Hughes's talent and reputation helped sell the film because of his role as writer and director, of course, but he made an impact as a result of the significant part he played in the marketing of and music choices within the film as well.

Marketing: the campaigns

Before Hughes came to Hollywood, he was a successful ad man, and he took this marketing training with him throughout his career as a filmmaker. He specifically focused his material on popular and populist content, did his own audience research, and had a say in how his films would be promoted. However, when he was at the beginning of his film career, and when his voice as a filmmaker keyed in to the pulse of the youth demographic was not yet established, he too had to deal with some adversarial studio executives who did not have faith in *The Breakfast Club*.

Either coincidentally because his preferences were in line with what was popular or purposefully because he studied his audience, the type of material Hughes chose to focus on was in line with contemporary audience tastes. Hughes himself said that he had 'no interest, none whatsoever, in doing something for [him]self instead of for the audience' (quoted in Carter 1991). He told Molly Ringwald, when she interviewed him for *Seventeen* magazine, that he preferred romance instead of ribald sex comedies (Ringwald 1986: 226); this penchant was consistent with research studies reported in *Variety* which found that youth at the time were interested in films that were 'passionately involving' instead of just sexual (Albert 1985). As he was making his teen films, Hughes said he realized how smart his young audience was, how much they liked serious material, and how conservative they were about sex (O'Connor 1986; Kelly 2001). The films Hughes made were well-timed to strike the right chords with contemporary youth.

In addition to his stated preferences, though, was also Hughes's aspiration of figuring out his audiences' desires and then satisfying them. From going to focus groups during his advertising days, he learned to pay attention to what people said they wanted. He also learned and thought to ask people, especially teens, about themselves in the first place. Sloane Tanen, the daughter of Ned Tanen, became his emissary of sorts into the teen mind. Hughes would call Sloane and ask her for pointers about what life was like for her, about what she thought of boys, and about what she thought of *Sixteen Candles* (Roberts 2016). He also had a long-running correspondence with a young female fan, Alison Byrne Fields, a girl for whom Hughes said in letters, 'I make these movies for you' (Byrne Fields 2009). According to Byrne Fields, Hughes had a sincere desire to tell young people's stories from their perspective, and their communication about her relationships with her parents and teachers helped him gain the necessary insights to do so. She was astute enough to realize that he was doing audience research but noted that she also liked to think that he really cared (ibid.).

Hughes's adolescent test market also included the teen actors with whom he worked. His long conversations with Molly Ringwald and Anthony Michael Hall helped him understand his target market, and when they would make recommendations and requests, he would often oblige (Honeycutt 2015; Roberts 2016). Hughes had a history of appeasing his audiences by altering his films; in a piece he wrote for *Zoetrope*, he noted that he changed the ending of *Vacation* to satisfy test audiences (Hughes 2008). Perhaps most famously (or notoriously, as people still debate which is better), because Ringwald and test audiences hated the original ending of *Pretty in Pink* that had Ringwald's character Andie end up with her friend Duckie (John Cryer) instead of her romantic interest Blane (Andrew McCarthy), the ending was reshot to have Andie and Blane together (Gora 2010: 143). This tendency came to bear on *The Breakfast Club* as well when, during shooting, after Ringwald, Sheedy, and co-producer Michelle Manning voiced their objections over a scene with a topless swim instructor, Hughes changed the role and wrote in a janitor instead. Meanwhile, Karen Leigh Hopkins, the actress originally cast as the swim instructor, recalls her role was more substantial instead of gratuitous and was devastated when it was cut for reasons she didn't understand (Hopkins 2015). Interestingly, all the versions of this story indicate how Hughes was trying to be all things to all people: have sentimentality and seriousness with one version of the role, include nudity that might be popular with studio executives and some audience segments with another, and change the role to placate his teenage consultants.

As tuned in to the teenage audience as he may have been, there were a few studio executives who thought Hughes actually did not know what he was doing with *The Breakfast Club* at all. Although Ned Tanen, former president of Universal Pictures, champion of filmmakers and teen films, and producer of *The Breakfast Club*, had faith in Hughes, he left in the middle of production to head Paramount's motion picture division. In charge of distributing the film instead was Frank Price, who became the new chair of the motion picture group at Universal, and Marvin Antonowsky, who was the head of marketing. Neither one liked the film; in fact, they supposedly hated it, and according to Tanen, they thought it was 'unreleasable' (quoted in Smith 1999: 145). Hughes remembered them saying that there was no story, 'no action, no party, no nudity,' and they did not think audiences would be interested in a film that was primarily just kids sitting around talking (Hughes, quoted in Smith 1999: 69).

Although the film has since become a touchstone, hearing the executives' comments is revelatory. It puts a different spin on what happens in *The Breakfast Club*, calling attention to some of the traditional teen film genre tropes the film does *not* contain. It also misses the point of what is considered 'story,' illustrates a lack of insight about audience tastes even in the midst of the teen film boom, and shows that even with extensive research, there are frequent surprises about what turns out to be a hit or miss with audiences. In addition, it places some of the new marketing practices being used in Hollywood into question, especially the ones that ask potential audiences what types of films they would like to see before an actual film is made or is in the early stages of development. Of course, the framing of the questions matters, but if test groups had been asked if they wanted to watch a group of teens 'sitting around talking in a group therapy session,' it is hard to imagine they would have been excited about the prospects.

As a result of the new Universal executives' attitude toward the film, unsurprisingly, they were tone-deaf when it came to marketing and promotion. Because they thought it was a commercial risk and were not convinced that teenagers would like it as it was, the original trailer they made positioned the film as a comedy with Chuck Berry music, the actors running through the halls, and Judd Nelson falling through the ceiling (Siskel 1985b; Smith 1999: 145). And going against what was becoming common practice at the time, they chose not to release 'Don't You (Forget About Me)' from the soundtrack ahead of the film's release, which would have drummed up more interest before the premiere. In the meeting when the studio executives revealed the original trailer footage to the filmmakers, Ned Tanen, who still had a say because he was producer and head of Channel Productions (one of the production companies behind *The Breakfast Club*), and had influence because of his clout in the industry, became livid. Michelle Manning reported that Tanen was so angry, 'if the table had not been bolted to the floor, Ned would have picked it up' (quoted in Smith 1999: 145). Eventually, the marketing campaign went to an advertising company instead where Howard Deutch, who would later direct *Pretty in Pink* and *Some Kind of Wonderful*, cut the trailers (Honeycutt 2015: 187). The story of that meeting is illustrative, though. It indicates that Hughes early in his career still needed someone else more powerful to back him, and it also demonstrates that studios were floundering when it came to understanding the target demographic for their movies. Even though teen films as a genre were popular at the time, there was no clear-cut formula for what would be successful.

The final trailer needed to accomplish a number of objectives – it had to publicize the personnel involved, identify the genre, match the film's comedic and dramatic tones, and indicate the story, which, as the studio executives pointed out, was lacking a great deal of exciting action and rarely leaves the confines of the library. Interestingly, instead of beginning with the teens or with any music cues, the trailer starts with Vernon in a low angle shot looking at his watch, telling the students how much time they have left to 'ponder the error of [their] ways.' There are then medium shots of all the teens sitting at their respective tables while he speaks, a cut back to Vernon asking if they have any questions, and then a shot of Bender sitting at one of the tables with his feet up, responding with 'Yeah, does Barry Manilow know that you raid his wardrobe?' From the very beginning, part of the story is signposted – the students are in a full-day detention at their high school. The teen film genre designation is made clear with the iconic genre images of teens sitting in the library, and with the generational conflict on display as the students are shown to be in direct opposition to Vernon, who appears to be the only adult present. The combination of both flippant and solemn tones is indicated as the dialogue switches between Vernon's hostility and Bender's joking and defiance. This switching back and forth between comedy and drama continues throughout the rest of the trailer – the shots of the teens being unruly are both lighthearted and serious. Bender falling through the ceiling and the five of them running through the halls, smoking pot, and dancing on the banister alternate with tougher rebelliousness, such as when Bender taunts Claire about how good it feels to be bad. The trailer also shifts between heavier emotional moments as the romantic couples kiss and Allison states that she does not want to be alone anymore (a line which is actually absent from the film), and lighter bonding, such as when the characters are all shown sitting on the floor laughing together.

As well as indicating genre, plot, and tone, the original theatrical trailer also clearly identifies key personnel. In line with the progression of the film, the teen characters are all introduced and initially labeled as types in voiceover with accompanying images of the actors playing their respective roles: 'a brain,' 'a beauty,' 'a jock,' 'a rebel,' and 'a recluse.' The voiceover then restates almost the exact same taglines and ad copy featured on the one-sheet: 'Before this day is over, they'll break the rules, bear their souls, take some chances, and touch each other in a way they never dreamed possible. *The Breakfast Club.* They only met once, but it changed their lives forever.' At the end, the studio (Universal Pictures) and then all of the actors are introduced, including Gleason, by last name in alphabetical order. The final credit states that *The Breakfast Club* is a John Hughes Film, before ending on a close-up of Molly Ringwald prior to the title and credits cards. As a piece of promotional material, the trailer does what it needs to do primarily by highlighting genre tropes of conflict and camaraderie, matching the film's lighter and more serious moments, and publicizing the talent – both the popular young actors and Hughes, who was gaining fame as a result of the success of *Sixteen Candles* released the year before.

Television commercials for the film take similar approaches to the theatrical trailer, but with some marked differences. Notably, the spots are shorter – 30 seconds to the trailer's 90 seconds – and so the messages need to be distilled. Interestingly, two commercials appearing at the time of the film's release both focus on story elements instead of paying as much attention to key personnel. The voiceover in one states, 'Their parents expect them to make good. Their school expects them to be bad. Nobody expects them to become friends, but that's just what they're gonna do.' The intercut scenes show the oppositions between the parents and the kids when they are dropping them off in front of the school, Vernon and Bender fighting, and the teens at odds with one another, before switching to focus on moments when the teens are smiling, talking, laughing, and dancing with one another. The voiceover in another commercial tells of 'Five strangers meeting for the first time. Five people with a talent for trouble. Five lives that will never be the same.' The intercut scenes feature Claire saying she's not going to discuss her personal life with strangers and then switches to demonstrate the students' solidarity when they cover for Bender after he falls through the ceiling and Vernon asks, 'What was that ruckus?' Afterward, it shows Bender and Claire kissing and Brian saying that he considers the others his friends, before ending with them all sitting on the floor and laughing. The first spot focuses on generational opposition and eventual peer group bonding while the second emphasizes the friendships formed over a transformative day.

When initially introducing the film and being limited for time, the commercials underscored the story elements. Meanwhile, a commercial advertising the television premiere of the film that aired two years later in 1987 took a different approach. After the film and its stars gained widespread recognition, the spot focused on more of the romantic couplings and running and dancing action, and identified only the young actors by name, this time in order of contemporary fame: Estevez, Ringwald, Nelson, Hall, and then Sheedy. The voiceover borrows directly from the original trailer: 'They only met once, but it changed their lives forever. *The Breakfast Club*.' In this instance, when pressed for time, the story is only briefly indicated, while the personnel are featured, signifying how important the young actors had become in such a short period of time and how their presence was a main selling point.

The commercials were an essential marketing tool for the film. Television spots were becoming especially important in the 1980s when the shift from print advertising was even more pronounced than in the previous decade. *Variety* reported in 1983 that contemporary youth audiences did not read many newspapers, nor did they rely heavily on critics' reviews when deciding on what films to watch, especially teen films (Goldberg 1983: 10). Additionally, because of the importance of synergy between films and soundtracks, studios were advertising films more heavily on MTV. MTV, which at the time of its premiere primarily showed video accompaniments to songs, had started broadcasting in 1981 (Goodwin 1992: 136). It quickly grew in popularity among youth audiences. It was also a network marketers looked toward when advertising teen films because the audiences for both MTV and the genre overlapped. The station was used to advertise films by airing music videos from the songs on the soundtracks but also did so by broadcasting trailers and commercials for the films. In 1985, reports in *Variety* stated that studios were increasing the number of commercials on MTV for teen films especially. At the time, the network was

> a significant force in reaching the hallowed 12–25 demographic . . . 'Vision Quest' has been the most heavily advertised of the pics in question on MTV, with Warner Bros. buying approximately 80 spots (half-30s and half-90s) over a 10–12 day period. In second place is 'The Breakfast Club' for which Universal has already bought 50–60 straight 30-second spots.
>
> (Gold 1985: 3)

While the trailers and commercials were crucial publicity tools central to the advertising campaigns, print materials were important as well. Promotional posters and production stills for the film abound. There are multiple versions of the five all leaning against lockers looking sullen in some and amused in others (see Figure 0.1 on page 3 of this book for a sample iteration of the oft-used pose). There are images of the five all sitting on a banister, looking alternately bored or in the middle of conversation. Still more materials circulate where the actors, out of their characters' costumes for the film, are featured together in different groupings. Meanwhile, others show John Hughes sitting with the actors, with some of them smiling and some of them serious, indicating their combination of comfort and discomfort in knowing exactly how they are supposed to behave and what vibe they are supposed to be embodying in the poses. The assorted images, evident when similar set-ups contrast with one another, illustrate the mix of tones the film was trying to achieve and show the variability of the dynamic between the actors – they were never in one constant mood throughout as single still images can belie. Even more so, they demonstrate how the marketing campaign captured an essential message of the film, that the characters, teens themselves, and the genre could not be pigeonholed, even if some members of older generations tried to do so.

Although a variety of images were produced, the one that stands out the most and is most closely associated with the film is the one-sheet (see the Frontispiece on the title page of this book). The main poster for the film was shot by famed photographer Annie Leibovitz toward the end of production. It appeared in print ads in newspapers and magazines, in theater lobbies and on promotional materials, and on the covers of the soundtrack and home video releases.

The taglines at the top and the character types identified by the actors' costumes, makeup, and hair tell of the film's plot. But the image does more, looking almost like an album cover instead of a one-sheet (Smith 1999: 76). Against a plain lavender background, all five actors are in an array of poses, so close together that they are almost on top of one another, overlapping, yet not touching. No one has more prominence than another; each is featured either because of being higher in the frame (Nelson), lying across the bottom (Ringwald), to the right but with a stark background (Estevez), in the center (Hall), or with the brightest lighting (Sheedy). What unites them is their look of defiance, boldly, unflinchingly meeting the camera without smiles, without coy looks off to the side, almost challenging the viewers to look back at them and then maybe to figure them out or leave them alone. The image itself does not focus on them looking at one another to show their closeness and newfound bonds – their alliance is pre-established. Rather, it shows them as a band of individuals, separate in their character types but unified as rebellious teenagers, against onlookers who would dare pass judgment. The *pièce de résistance* of the marketing campaign, the one-sheet captures the essence of the film.

Marketing: the music

An essential element of *The Breakfast Club*, both in terms of its content and its marketing, is the music. Music was used to set the tone and mood, to set the pace of action, to convey plot and enhance narrative moments, and to speak for the characters' emotional states. The soundtrack also featured New Wave music; Hughes was an avid fan of the genre, and by putting it in his films, helped popularize it in the US (Gora 2010: 160). As a marketing tool, there was cross-promotion via the soundtrack and music videos, and by the songs featured in trailers and commercials. In fact, music is so important to the film that it opens with a quote from David Bowie's song 'Changes': 'And these children that you spit on as they try to change their worlds are immune to your consultations. They're quite aware of what they're going through.' As another indication of the close collaboration between Hughes and his cast, Ally Sheedy reported that she recommended Bowie's song to Hughes during production and was later surprised when, at her first screening of the film, she saw the quote in the opening sequence. When interviewed for the Special Features on *The Breakfast Club, 25th Anniversary* DVD (2010), she said it was one of her proudest moments.

In the 1980s, the extensive use of music in films and marketing was a primary way filmmakers incorporated the concept of synergy into practice. This synergy was especially effective with teen films and teen audiences because the youth market had a high rate of spending on film and music ('Youth Barometer' 1985: 2) and because the youth demographic was the primary target of both media (Litwak 1986: 244). One of the most effective tools that combined the film and music experience was the soundtrack, and as such, films would often be released with an accompanying soundtrack album. The music would underscore key moments in the film itself, but then those music moments could be capitalized upon in publicity and sales of the related album. The music on the soundtrack, and the music in trailers, commercials, and music videos, would all enhance awareness and increase brand recognition, where the 'brand' equals the film. As Jeff Smith points out in *The Sounds of Commerce: Marketing Popular Music*, even if there were debates about whether the film sold the music or vice versa, it barely mattered because both benefitted from the success of the other (1998: 58).

Key in the cross-promotion process was MTV, which had just started broadcasting a few years before *The Breakfast Club* was released. Although its audience was small, it was the same demographic targeted by the film and music industries. As a result, its place in marketing strategies grew in importance rapidly over the course of the decade. With its music-centered programming, the channel was an ideal marketing tool that would target the youth demographic by featuring visual accompaniment to modern songs and video images of contemporary performers, along with music tie-ins to popular movies. It followed quickly that music videos would be an essential tool in advertising soundtracks. Short clips from already made films could be used in conjunction with shots of the performers to create the music video. Although there had to be enough footage so audiences could identify from which film the song and video came, a few years into broadcasting, MTV stipulated that less than 50% of the music video come from the film, lest it look too blatantly like commercial advertising (Epstein 1984: 16). The release of soundtrack videos was timed to coordinate with publicity for the film, and all together, the films and music videos would feed into one another to increase exposure, awareness, and sales. Because of *The Breakfast Club*'s status as a teen film, with its majority youth audience that was presumed to go along with it, music played a prominent role in both the content and marketing.

In another complementary match between film, filmmaker, and time of production, Hughes was known for his voracious and eclectic music tastes and stressed the importance of music to his films. Hughes had such an extensive record collection that he had an entire room in his house dedicated to his holdings. His love of music was shared by the young actors with whom he worked. It strengthened their bonds and reinforced the way Hughes was able to relate to youth audiences. Hughes and the cast, especially Ringwald and Hall, would share music they liked and discovered by exchanging mix tapes and going to concerts together, and Hughes would write screenplays with music as inspiration – 'Pretty in Pink' was a song by the Psychedelic Furs that Ringwald gave Hughes during filming of *The Breakfast Club* (Ringwald 2009; Gora 2010: 161; Kamp 2010b; Honeycutt 2015: 73). Further reinforcing the prominence of music to *The Breakfast Club*, Hughes said,

> I started [thinking about the music] when I was still writing the script. I wanted it to be heavy on the drums and bass because there were clocks ticking and emotions ticking. I chose Keith Forsey [as the composer] because he was a drummer. Keith came in and watched rehearsal, talked to the actors, and 'Don't You (Forget About Me)' was what he took away from it.
>
> (quoted in Smith 1999: 145–146)

Effectively, Hughes brought music to all stages of filmmaking, including pre- and post-production.

In addition to Hughes's statements, the prominent role music played in *The Breakfast Club* is evident through everything from the production companies to key personnel. A&M, the first company that put up money for *The Breakfast Club*, was even better known as a record company, and Universal, the distributor, was owned by MCA – also a music company. Ned Tanen, one of the producers of the film through his company Channel Productions, as president of Universal Pictures was known for greenlighting youth-oriented fare that also had best-selling soundtracks like *American Graffiti* (1973) and *Fast Times at Ridgemont High* (1982). David Anderle was the music supervisor and recommended Forsey because of his work on 'Flashdance . . . What a Feeling,' a recent hit soundtrack song. Costume Designer Marilyn Vance was influenced by Chrissie Hynde of the band The Pretenders for both Bender's and Allison's wardrobes. All of these connections came to bear on getting Simple Minds to record the hit song 'Don't You (Forget

About Me)' for *The Breakfast Club* soundtrack. The band did not want to make the song – one composed by someone else for what they thought was just another teen film. However, they were encouraged by Chrissie Hynde herself (lead singer Jim Kerr's wife at the time) and then more forcefully urged by Ned Tanen, who convinced Gil Friesen at A&M that this was the band they needed (Honeycutt 2015: 81). As chance would have it, A&M was the production company and also Simple Minds' record label.

While Hughes and Tanen were essential for getting key personnel aboard, it was Hughes whose tastes informed the kind of music used for the film. This was especially notable with his penchant for bands that were not well known and for New Wave music. Going against current soundtrack strategies that often tried to incorporate a big-named act to help promote the album and film, Hughes would tap into more obscure talent and use the film as a platform to introduce the band and the songs to wider audiences. This tactic seemed to increase his credibility in the music industry – instead of his use of music appearing like an afterthought or an advertising ploy, he was commended for being a 'legitimate practitioner' of the synergy model (Denisoff and Romanowski 1991: 591), and he was recognized as one of the only filmmakers to land his own record label deal after the success of soundtracks for his films (Goldstein 1987). Indeed, the songs do complement the action and pace of the film at multiple points. The music is especially notable when the five students are running through the halls following Bender while trying to avoid Vernon to the tune of Wang Chung's 'Fire in the Twilight' with the lyrics 'hot on the run from the grip of the power game, the man who leads the way.' It is also evident during the montage sequence when, at the end of their day of bonding, they all dance to Karla DeVito's 'We Are Not Alone' after Brian puts the record on in the library. While the dance montage seems a bit dated and emblematic of common trends in films of the decade because of the influence of the MTV aesthetic, the lyrics and rhythm of the songs still highlight and heighten both emotional release and narrative currents.

The montage set to DeVito's 'We Are Not Alone' with the teens dancing by themselves all over the library and then together on the banister in various groupings became famous. Although there was no music video for the song, clips from the sequence were used extensively in commercials and in the trailer. It is the moment where the film operates most obviously in the musical mode, an especially important defining element of the teen film as a genre. In *The Breakfast Club*, and in many teen films especially from the time, teens purposefully choose the music they are engaging with, in essence identifying *with* music as opposed to being identified *by* music, where the former indicates an active role and the latter a passive role (Nelson 2011: 253). By framing the use of music in this way, by having the characters choose what music they are going to listen to and what they are going to do while it is playing, the teens are able to express themselves. In effect, by using music in films this way, the characters can express emotions they might not otherwise be able to in dialogue, and they become empowered – they choose the soundtrack of their own lives. That the music was chosen by Hughes with reported influence from his young cast helps support this assertion.

Hughes's tastes informed the sounds for his films and as such, his soundtracks are populated with New Wave music. 1980s New Wave grew out of 1970s punk, but the music was considered 'more stylish and accessible' (Cateforis 2014: 10). New Wave is an umbrella term for music that is composed of pop-type sounds that 'weren't part of the mainstream, yet were melodic, catchy, idiosyncratic and quirky' (Erlewine 2002: 1338). The New Wave sound and many of the bands' tendencies toward modern aesthetics were an especially good fit for MTV videos. Additionally, the often sentimental lyrics complemented Hughes's storytelling to create both a 'commercial synergy' and an 'emotional synergy' that enhanced the connection between the music and the films (Gora 2010: 157). This connection was most notable with Simple Minds' 'Don't You (Forget About Me),' the song used at the beginning and end of the film and the one most closely associated with *The Breakfast Club*. The drumbeat and the lyrics literally intone the theme and hope of the film, that the five will remain friends when Monday comes, even though it remains a question at the film's end. The raw emotions in the film are matched by those in the song – 'Will you recognize me? Call my name or walk on by' – along with the title request repeated throughout: 'Don't you, forget about me.'

The song was a huge success, even if the rest of the album was not. 'Don't You (Forget About Me)' is immediately evocative of *The Breakfast Club* and serves as an anthem of sorts not only for the film but for teen films of the era as well. It was in heavy rotation on MTV, and although there were less than 30 seconds of footage from the film shown only on small television screens in the over four-minute-long video (see Figure 4.1), it was definitively linked with the film. Whereas 'Fire in the Twilight,' the other soundtrack music video, contained more footage and even had a Ringwald cameo, 'Don't You' was the one used extensively in the commercials (although interestingly, not in the trailer). Based largely on the popularity of the Simple Minds' song, which reached number one and was on the charts for 22 weeks (Denisoff and Romanowski 1991: 486), the soundtrack reached number seven on *Billboard*'s Top Soundtrack Albums of 1985 ('The '80s Soundtracks' 1989). The album as a whole, though, was not received as well as the lead track. Four of the ten songs were instrumentals, and the album was criticized for being 'aesthetically rather weak' (Denisoff and

Figure 4.1 The video for 'Don't You (Forget About Me)' contains very little foot-age of the film, and what is visible is seen only through small television screens.

Romanowski 1991: 486); Robert Christgau, music critic for *The Village Voice*, wrote at the time of release that it was 'utterly negligible' (1985).

The strength of 'Don't You (Forget About Me)' is formidable though. To date, it remains Simple Minds' only number one hit and is the song most closely associated with the band as well as the film. Emphasizing the importance and the intertwining of the music and the marketing, Universal used the song extensively in commercials, ones that were often in rotation on MTV, because they 'recognized the statistical reality that 68 percent of music video viewers chose a movie to see as a result of cable exposure. Music trailers *did* serve as ideal scouts for teen-oriented film and music makers' (Denisoff and Romanowski 1991: 489). And noting the lasting impact of both the film and the song, music critic Stephen Thomas Erle-wine called 'Don't You (Forget About Me)' an 'undisputed masterpiece' and 'the sound of the mid-'80s, without exception' (no date). *The Breakfast Club* offered a marriage of the music and the marketing, weaving together

Hughes's tastes with the narrative and the film's tone, and mixing musical moments that grew organically from the film with successful marketing strategies capitalizing on contemporary styles. While certainly of the New Wave and teen film moments of the 1980s, the way the music was used, and specifically the song 'Don't You (Forget About Me),' endures. When commenting on the effect of the music Hughes used on his soundtracks, Todd Martens in the *Los Angeles Times* went so far as to say that 'if the boomers had Woodstock, Generation X had John Hughes' (2009).

Conclusion

Hughes's savvy and marketing acumen carried over not just to the content of the film, including the narrative and the music, but to the content of the ad lines to which he also contributed. Furthermore, he had a carefully crafted strategy around the release dates of his teen films:

> I'm growing a market: 'Sixteen Candles' will come out on videocassette as 'The Breakfast Club' is opening. 'Breakfast Club' will be on cassette as 'Pretty in Pink' is coming. It created this wave. It took three years to get through it. And it worked. Those pictures are worth a lot of money. They're going to be worth a lot in the future because they play endlessly and they're a valuable part of somebody's catalogue. They rent consistently. A girl turns 16, she rents 'Sixteen Candles.' It's the No. 1 pajama party movie. And every four years there's a whole new crop of teen-agers. And then again in 20 years it's going to be their nostalgia. And their kids are going to watch. It's going to be like Andy Hardy.
>
> (quoted in Carter 1991)

This plan, while decidedly calculated, shows how the 'Molly trilogy,' as Corliss labeled it in *Time* in 1986, served both Hughes's interests as a filmmaker trying to create material of interest to himself and his audiences, and illustrated his shrewd business acumen. In this light, the serious nature of *The Breakfast Club* can be seen to have deliberate cross-generational interest, not just youth appeal, as older generations can watch to remind themselves what it was like when they were younger. It is difficult to say if this plan was solidified more in retrospect than at the time of production. The article was written in 1991, the year after Hughes's biggest success, *Home Alone*, was released and four years after the release of his last teen film *Some Kind of Wonderful* in 1987. He had hoped that Ringwald would star in *Wonderful* as well, but she declined because she thought the material was too similar to their previous collaborations, a rejection which seemed to be the cause of the rift between them. Thinking of these four films together (*Sixteen, Breakfast, Pink,* and *Wonderful*), along with *Ferris Bueller's Day Off* (*Weird Science* appears to be an anomaly that Hughes himself called a 'dopey-assed comedy' (Smith 1999: 145) that he did not like very much), a repeated dynamic becomes evident. There are romantic couplings and one odd person out in all of them. Hughes was often reported to have written autobiographical stories with different themes and variations. Whether he felt like the insider or the outsider – when he was part of a couple or an interloper, a member of a popular group or an outcast – he mined various versions of his own life for his films. For four years from 1984 to 1987, coincidentally the same length of time as high school, his background as an adolescent and as an ad man, and his interests as a filmmaker, helped him synchronize his teen tales and marketing strategies with his target audience.

5   The lasting legacy

Historical reception, contemporary impact, and Hughes as auteur

By the 1990s, writers were already looking back on and characterizing the 1980s, seeing it as a decade with a particular personality and with a set of qualities ranging from Reaganomics to MTV, yuppies to shoulder pads, that made it unique. The abundance of teen films, and John Hughes's close association with the genre, are part of what demarcate the era. Hughes, who directed eight films, produced 23, and wrote over 30 (including ones written under pen names), actually only made six teen films, of which he directed only four. Yet, he is widely associated with the genre, and *The Breakfast Club* is considered the archetypical specimen. In *Totally Awesome 80s: A Lexicon of the Music, Videos, Movies, TV Shows, Stars, and Trends of That Decadent Decade*, Matthew Rettenmund pronounces the film the 'ultimate 80s movie' based on factors including recognizability and memorability; characteristically '80s elements, such as Brat Pack cast members and number one hits on its soundtrack; and its impact, gauged by the imitations it inspired, and says ultimately that *The Breakfast Club* is 'one of the most important and moving teen films of all time and the quintessential moviegoing experience of the 80s' (1996: 78 and 80).

However, the film's road to exemplary status and Hughes's exaltations as an auteur were not initially so smooth and steadfast. Although *The Breakfast Club* was a box-office success when it was released, indicating its approval from audiences, it originally had a mixed critical response, and it was lauded only after it proved its durability in the home market. Indeed, the film was released at an opportune time to engender its staying power. By the mid-1980s, both cable and VHS were becoming popular platforms for watching films, and *The Breakfast Club* was a broadcast and video staple. Because of the industrial moment in which it was created, its constant replay led to its familiarity and its widespread and deep-rooted impact, especially on young audiences growing up with the film. Importantly, though, it is unlikely to have been aired and watched repeatedly had it not also had inherent appeal and enduring quality, something that spoke to the generation and the larger young adult population represented in the film.

In the middle of production, Hughes's fellow Chicagoan film critic Robert Ebert came to visit the set. After observing filming and speaking with the cast and crew, he stated that 'during a break in the shooting I began to pick up those particular vibes you get on the sets of movies that might very well turn out to be special' (1984). His reflections were prescient. Years later, after the film and Hughes had grown in esteem, realizing the enormity of what he accomplished, Hughes himself stated, 'I think I was able to get at something immutable, and I'm proud that it has lasted. I was desperately afraid of getting it wrong. It's really about characters and what they have to say. I've spent 15 years looking for that again' (quoted in Smith 1999: 146).

Hughes would not get the chance to find it again. He moved on from teen films, then moved away from Hollywood and filmmaking, and died suddenly in 2009. When he passed away, the reactions were visceral and the accolades profuse. In a series of articles in *Vanity Fair* written after he died, David Kamp explained why the response was so profound, emphasizing how the films 'transcended their origins' and became 'loadstars' for future filmmakers:

> [H]is movies turned out to be a renewable resource, with a reach far beyond the generation for which they were originally intended ... when Hughes died suddenly of a heart attack while out walking in New York City last August, at only 59 years of age, it wasn't just the 25th-reunion crowd that fell into mourning and remembrance but nearly the whole of movie-watching America.
>
> (Kamp 2010b)

Very few filmmakers are able to reach audiences in such ways, as evinced by the special Oscar tribute given to Hughes in 2010.

The initial reception and ongoing reevaluations of *The Breakfast Club* and John Hughes are the subjects of this concluding chapter. And while Hughes's significance is striking, it is also important to keep in mind the context of production of his films and note that as influential as *The Breakfast Club* remains, it is part of a larger genre that was experiencing a resurgence during the decade. Some of the reasons the film has endured in particular though are because of the voice Hughes gave the characters and the weight he gave the story. The film brings together genre-defining elements – the conflicts between generations and peer pressure, archetypical characters and breaking down stereotypes to reveal the people underneath, the celebration and survival of adolescence, and the importance of this time in life on the coming-of-age process – to become a distinctive moment for Hughes the filmmaker and for teen films in the 1980s. Its endurance speaks to the way the film's level of importance as a critical, commercial, and influential film with tremendous impact has grown since its initial debut.

Box office, business, and influence

The Breakfast Club had a wide release in over 1,100 theaters on Presidents' Day weekend, February 15, 1985, and had the highest opening of the films premiering that week. On a budget between $6 and 9 million, more than its initial $1 million when it was at A&M but still on the low end for a major studio picture (Tusher 1985; Smith 1999: 69), it went on to earn almost $46 million at the domestic box office and an additional $5.5 million internationally. Hughes's second outing as a director was the 16th highest grossing film of 1985 and the third highest R-rated film of the year (boxofficemojo.com). It marked the beginning of an auspicious streak that ran from 1985 to 1991. After the success of *Home Alone*, Hughes was ranked seventh among top producers, with his films earning a cumulative box-office gross of almost $765 million (Frook 1992).

Success was not just at the box office. *The Breakfast Club* video was the second highest seller in the first month of its release in September 1985, went on to be #48 in video rentals for the remainder of the year, and #12 in video rentals the following year (Bierbaum 1985; '1985: The Year in Music & Video' 1985; '1986: The Year in Music & Video' 1986). Three years after its theatrical release, it still had high ratings when shown on television ('Local Election' 1988: 22), and in May 2003, a reissue of the DVD, 19 years after the film's release (not a special edition), charted at #39 of *Billboard*'s Top DVD Sales ('Top DVD Sales' 2003: 51). When teen films were again popular at the box office in the late 1990s, in a retrospective article about the film in *Premiere* magazine (and one of Hughes's last interviews on record), Sean Smith (1999) reported that more than a million videos had been sold nationwide. That number has increased considering all the reissues of the film since then, many of which contain new special features, including the Flashback, 25th and 30th Anniversary, Universal's 100th Anniversary, and various Blu-ray editions. It has also been bundled with other films in packages, such as the '80s Comedies Spotlight, John Hughes Yearbook, Brat Pack, and High School Reunion collections. In 2018, there was even a Criterion Collection (a prestige home video distributor) DVD release that featured restorations, commentary, interviews, documentaries, and almost an hour of footage that had never before been released.

Illustrating its perpetual popularity, commercial viability, and sustained interest from audiences, the ongoing presence of the film in popular culture is not just about new video releases, which have been plentiful, or theatrical re-releases on anniversaries. There continue to be hundreds of film, television, and popular culture references to *The Breakfast Club*. These connections to the film vary from direct references to the film or the song 'Don't You (Forget About Me),' homages, recreated scenes and images (especially Bender's fist pump and the iconic one-sheet), borrowed storylines and premises, satires and spoofs (sometimes with actors from the film), and characters who refer directly to socially segmented groupings similar to the ones that were first explicitly laid out in *The Breakfast Club*. Sample titles include *Clueless* (Heckerling 1995), *Dogma* (Smith 1999), *Not Another Teen Movie*, *Mean Girls* (Waters 2004), *Easy A* (Gluck 2010), *Pitch Perfect* (Moore 2012), and *The DUFF* (Sandel 2015). Television shows, especially ones with articulate teens delving into emotional material like *My So-Called Life* (1994–95), *Dawson's Creek* (1998–2003), and *The O.C.* (2003–07) also bear the mark of the film. Even documentaries and reality shows like *American Teen* (Burstein 2008) and *If You Really Knew Me* (2010) use *The Breakfast Club* narrative as influence to investigate high school cliques. Nostalgia films and shows that go back to the 1980s, such as *Romy and Michelle's High School Reunion* (Mirkin 1997) and *Freaks and Geeks* (1999–2000), recreate not just the decade, but the time period as depicted in Hughes's films and the types of characters found in high schools that he articulated in *The Breakfast Club*.

The critics, the fans

Although audiences were quick to praise and popularize *The Breakfast Club*, media makers continually reference it, and the film has grown in esteem, the initial critical reception was actually rather mixed. For instance, in 2016, the film was added to the National Film Registry, a designation for showcasing 'the range and diversity of American film heritage to increase awareness for its preservation' (Kreps 2016). When it was released, Universal ran a 'For Your Consideration' advertisement in *Variety* asking Academy voters to consider nominating the film in the categories of best picture, director, supporting actors and actresses, editing, and song, but it did not receive any nominations ('For Your Consideration' 1985).

Meanwhile many contemporary reviews were double-edged – they would commend Hughes for his ability to write from a teen perspective but then criticize the subject matter as merely puerile protests that do not really matter. For example, famed *New Yorker* critic Pauline Keal and *New York Times* reviewer Janet Maslin were in agreement, both about *The Breakfast Club* when it was released and when they were looking back on the film and Hughes after *Pretty in Pink*: Hughes always stayed with the teens' point of view, would not be condescending, and would aim for understanding the characters (Kael 1989; Maslin 1987: 21). But these were not necessarily compliments because the characters he understood so well were young. Maslin asserted that he treats their concerns 'as if they were matters of state' (ibid.) and that while he had a 'talent for casting,' the actors were forced into 'fraudulent encounter-group candor' (1985). Kael declared that 'the movie is about a bunch of stereotypes who complain that other people see them as stereotypes' and 'appeals to young audiences by blaming adults for the kids' misery' (1985). Mixed reviews were not just about the content but also about the actors. Some critics applauded the cast, either in toto or individual members, but not everyone agreed whom to praise or deride. For example, Sheedy was alternately a 'marvelous comic sprite' (ibid.) or 'overwrought and seemingly amateurish' (Byrge 1985); Nelson either 'overplays the punk' ('Picks and Pans' 1985) or 'creates the strong center of the film' (Ebert 1985).

Some of the more glaring negative reviews came from the industry trade papers. Again, the compliments would be backhanded by saying teens may like the film, implying therefore that it must not really be very good. *Variety* claimed that although it might 'pass as deeply profound among today's teenage audience,' the characters do not 'have anything intelligent to say' and just 'whine and complain' ('The Breakfast Club' 1985: 19). *The Hollywood Reporter* likened it to detention itself, 'a grim and dull experience,' but did note that it at least ventured beyond the formulaic (Byrge 1985). More lukewarm reviews in *People* labeled the film 'The Little Chill' ('Picks and Pans' 1985), likening the film to *The Big Chill* (Kasdan 1983) except with teens having the personal revelations instead of adults. Again, the importance of the teen experience is minimized.

Some initial reviews, though, for example from popular critics Gene Siskel and Roger Ebert, were more positive. Ebert (1985) wrote Hughes tried to create plausible teenagers (acknowledging that his weakness was adult characters), and Siskel (1985a) appreciated how well the 'confessional formula' worked, writing Hughes is 'a savvy chronicler of contemporary teenage life.' Siskel's review was so glowing, his line that the film is 'a breath of cinematic fresh air' was used for ad copy in *Variety*. More admiring reviews followed when Molly Ringwald landed on the cover of *Time* the following year with Richard Corliss noting that *The Breakfast Club* and *Sixteen Candles* before it 'succeed because they are about the kids who go to see them . . . They are also funny movies, finely crafted and boasting spectacular ensemble acting' (1986).

Before the hagiographies written after Hughes's death in 2009, there were a number of writers who realized that additional critical distance was needed to gauge his films, that likely because his films were so popular, he would not be more fully appreciated until time had passed. In 1991, after the release of *Home Alone*, director Chris Columbus stated about Hughes that 'critics can only fight the American public for so long,' and writer Neal Gabler said in the future, 'people will talk about how he synthesized culture, how he spoke for the society in the middle of the country' (quoted in Carter 1991). Scholar Robert Sklar was also complimentary, writing,

> When future histories from lengthier hindsight rank the significant figures of 1980s Hollywood, it will be interesting to see whether Hughes holds a place among Spielberg and Lucas, Stallone and Schwarzenegger, and others whose artistry may rise to greater prominence as box-office triumph fades.
>
> (Sklar 1994: 347)

Their predictions were correct. When the film was re-released in theaters to coincide with yet another DVD edition on the 30th anniversary, some sources took to publishing their original, more negative reviews to show they realized they did not completely understand the film and how opinions can change, especially with the benefit of time and the film's apparent longevity. *Newsday* reported in 1985 that the film was 'nothing you haven't heard before' and was only 'slightly more interesting than one might expect' (Gelmis 1985). In 2015, the same source called it 'a cultural touchstone for several generations and a landmark for movies overall' and said that the film 'remains as relevant and youthful as ever' (Guzmán 2015). Kirk Honeycutt, whose book on Hughes also came out in 2015, originally said in the *Los Angeles Daily News* that he 'thought the movie was a little pat, a little too eager to blame the parents, then go home,' but then reconsidered:

> A lot of critics didn't treat (Hughes) fairly . . . These kid problems looked overblown. We missed the relevance. Hughes was making a point about how it felt to be a teen, and we missed it with 'Breakfast Club.' I failed it too. But then, a good film – you see something new each time. And 30 years later, I've changed my mind.
>
> (quoted in Borrelli 2015)

Although initial critical reviews were mixed, and subsequent published reviews were mostly laudatory, many enthusiastic fan responses were immediate, lasting, and passionate. Co-producer Michelle Manning said she went to a theater when the film first came out with some of the filmmakers and the cast who sneaked in after the lights went down. She remembers that 'these kids [in the audience] were just going wild for the movie . . . And I just went, "Oh my God, they *get* the movie." What we were saying in that marketing meeting was true – these kids could totally relate' (Gora 2010: 80). Hughes himself reported in 1986 that he got 'a tremendous amount of mail from kids about the movies,' between 3,000 and 4,000 letters just about *The Breakfast Club* (O'Connor 1986), and according to the building manager of the old Maine North High School in Des Plaines, Illinois, which now holds official state offices, about 30 people a summer are still begging to see the film's shooting location (Borrelli 2015). In 2001, a *Salon* contributor wrote that she revered Hughes and the film 'to this day for being the first filmmaker who connected with me on a personal level, with an insight into my every-day thoughts, worries and experiences, and for being the only movie person to capture what it was like to be an adolescent in the '80s' (Kelly 2001). Showing some of the film's international influence, a contributor to UK's *The Independent* wrote that 'John Hughes was the auteur of adolescence, and *The Breakfast Club* was his finest moment' (Manzoor 2004). Contemporary and current reactions indicate the film's vast reach and extensive impact, reaffirming how audiences then and now identify with different characters and feel connected to the story.

Of course, picking out superlative responses does not mean some negative comments are without merit or that the film is now universally loved, but they do attest to its lasting power and how it has remained in ongoing cultural conversations. While problems such as its noticeable gender issues and lack of diversity are more obvious as sentiments have changed in the decades since the film's release, criticisms in hindsight are still valid, even if understood to be out of the historical context in which the film was made. And even if there are different opinions about the quality of the acting and whether the kids are just complainers, the point of valorizations of the film are less about extolling a magnum opus and more about realizing what the film was able to accomplish: instead of seeing the film as solely about the silly problems of teens and thinking that neither the problems nor the teens matter, *The Breakfast Club* is about seeing the world from the teens' perspective, acknowledging that their problems are real, and saying that they do matter. At the time, taking up the tales of Generation X teens from their point of view was just beginning to become more widespread.

The Breakfast Club connected with the teen experience certainly, and Hughes is one of the filmmakers responsible not just for bringing teens and their perspective to the screen but also for helping popularize and legitimize the teen film genre. However, it's important to note that the film and the film-maker were part of a significantly larger movement in filmmaking. Indeed, the 1980s was one of the most prolific periods of teen film production, and many of the films took various kinds of teen issues seriously or tried to get at the teen experience in a way that resonated with youth audiences. Many of the qualities Hughes and *The Breakfast Club* are lauded for were apparent in other films also, released either before or contemporaneously: *Fast Times at Ridgemont High* is told from the teens' point of view and is primarily a young woman's story; *Valley Girl* (Coolidge 1983) captured teen dialogue, cross-clique romance, and contained New Wave music; *The Outsiders* segments high school social groups by class; *Revenge of the Nerds* (Kanew 1984) and *The Karate Kid* have unpopular teens as the heroes; *Footloose* portrays generational conflicts; *Back to the Future* describes the importance of high school events, showing how adults got to be who they are by depicting them as teens; and *Better Off Dead* (Holland 1985) imagines characters with rich inner lives and crushes, as well as the social hierarchies of high school. These and other films from the era give context to the combination of circumstances in which *The Breakfast Club* was produced – this was a time when filmmakers were paying attention to the youth market and trying to appeal to it by telling teen stories with the teen perspective in mind. Holding up *The Breakfast Club* as exemplary does not diminish the other films. Rather, it states that the film represented teen voices and teen life in a particularly effective, enduring way, and that it contained so many fundamental teen film elements, from the larger genre and from the 1980s specifically. Arguably, Hughes is one of the reasons the genre coalesced at the time – he tapped into the essential nature of the teen film and helped formulate much of what has come to be expected from it.

Hughes as auteur

In the immediate aftermath of *The Breakfast Club*, Hughes went on to make *Weird Science* and *Ferris Bueller's Day Off*, and the latter film, along with *Sixteen Candles* and *The Breakfast Club*, have been called his 'teen trilogy.' The 'puberty-on-film trilogy' as Anthony Michael Hall (quoted in Gora 2010: 237) called his collaborations with Hughes, includes *Sixteen*, *Breakfast*, and *Weird*, and the 'Molly trilogy' includes *Sixteen*, *Breakfast*, and *Pretty in Pink*, the film released in 1986, which Hughes wrote but enlisted Howard Deutch, who cut the trailer for *Breakfast Club*, to direct. His last teen film in 1987, which marked the first soundtrack that came out under Hughes Music, his own record label at MCA, was *Some Kind of Wonderful*, another he wrote but Deutch directed. Noticeably, the storyline of two people vying for the affection of another, mixed with conflicts around popularity and class disparity, were similar between *Sixteen*, *Pink*, and *Wonderful*, but the last was without his red-haired muse, and *Pink*, as well as *Ferris*, were without the maturing Michael (Hall's given first name and what he prefers to be called). Both Ringwald and Hall had falling outs with Hughes after wanting to broaden their range and work with other filmmakers (Ringwald 2009; Kamp 2010a; Kamp 2010b); Hughes even cut off almost all contact with both of them after they made their last films together. For all his popularity as a filmmaker, Hughes had a well-known reputation as someone who held on to grudges, was easily offended and difficult to work with, and had notoriously closed off contact with many of his former stars and fellow crew members even after once being so close (Lallch 1993).

Hughes moved on from making teen films and shifted to family-oriented comedies, some more successful than others. He had a couple box-office misfires with *She's Having a Baby* (1988) and *Curly Sue* (1991), the last film he directed. Some of his subsequent hits, like *Planes, Trains & Automobiles* (Hughes 1987) and *Uncle Buck* (Hughes 1989), starred John Candy, another actor with whom he had a close relationship but whose early death in 1994 was disheartening to him and precipitated his departure from Hollywood. His principal fortunes were actually made in even younger-oriented fare from writing and producing *Home Alone* and *101 Dalmatians* (Herek 1996). After the phenomenal success of *Home Alone*, he had enough clout to move back to the Midwest, where he always wanted to stay, and have his own production company based in Chicago called Hughes Entertainment. Occasionally, he would write screenplays like *Beethoven* (Levant 1992) under the pseudonym Edmond Dantès or have stories produced based on his ideas, such as *Maid in Manhattan* (Wang 2002) or *Drillbit Taylor* (Brill 2008), both released under his pen name. But by the mid-1990s, he was largely absent from Hollywood, and by the early 2000s, he was absent from active filmmaking, leaving people to label him a Generation X J. D. Salinger (Ringwald 2009) after the reclusive author who wrote the coming-of-age classic *The Catcher in the Rye* (1951) and then receded from public view.

Hughes himself may have disappeared from Hollywood, but his films and influence remained. During the resurgence of the teen film in the late 1990s, *Premiere* ran a feature on Hughes and *The Breakfast Club* called 'Teen Days that Shook the World' (Smith 1999), highlighting the far-reaching impact of the film and the moment of which it was a part. In 2003, *Variety* reported that 'A decade after John Hughes vanished into the mists of the Reagan era . . . the Zeitgeist is shifting in Hughes's favor,' and noted his influence on new filmmakers who were raised on his films in the '80s (Bing 2003). And a year before he died, a feature in the *Los Angeles Times* asserted that his 'imprint remains':

> John Hughes hasn't set foot in Hollywood for years, but his influence has never been more potent . . . he has an entire generation of fans in the industry who grew up infatuated with his films, especially a string of soulful mid-1980s teen comedies that helped capture the eternal drama of modern teenage existence.
>
> (Goldstein 2008)

Fans, their interest, and Hughes's withdrawal sparked a documentary *Don't You Forget About Me* (Sadowski and Sadowski 2009) and a memoir, *Searching for John Hughes* (2016), which details Jason Diamond's quests for trying (unsuccessfully) to find the elusive filmmaker. People could take walking tours of Hughes's film sites in Chicago, but with his house in the suburbs and his farm in western Illinois, they were unlikely to see him.

Articles about the influence of Hughes, *The Breakfast Club*, and the Brat Pack actors who starred in it have been numerous and consistent since the film's release, but there were flurries of commentaries on the 30th anniversary. *Rolling Stone* reported that 'virtually every creator and consumer of adolescent-focused entertainment in the three decades since the film's debut owes a huge debt of gratitude to Hughes for turning teenagers into young adults' (Wood 2015). Indeed, media makers like Kevin Smith, Judd Apatow, Paul Feig, John Singleton, Diablo Cody, Josh Schwartz, Stephanie Savage, Tom Vaughan, and more have all stated that Hughes had a direct impact on their work (Schneller 2007; Goldstein 2008; Wood 2015; Kamp 2018), with Smith even saying that 'Basically my stuff is just John Hughes films with four-letter words' (quoted in Goldstein 2008). Hughes's effect on filmmaking extends beyond teen media; his method of keeping the cameras rolling as actors improvised on set, which got attention with reports that he shot over a million feet of film on *The Breakfast Club*, 'has become virtually an industry standard' style of shooting comedy (Goldstein 2008). Initial critical responses to his oeuvre may have been mixed, but the kids who grew up watching his films became media makers in their own right who used what they learned from him, and they were quick to acknowledge the meaningful impressions he made.

Although Hughes's films never left the popular culture conversation, perhaps the most fervent period of writing about Hughes and his influence occurred after he passed away suddenly from a heart attack at the age of 59 in 2009. Even though he had removed himself from Hollywood and filmmaking for years, the permanent absence of his death left a profound impact. Writers expressed their deep sorrow, as though a personal figure in their lives had died, and his status as an affecting auteur, as an artist with a distinct and extensive reach was repeated in myriad ways. Ebert said that 'few directors have left a more distinctive or influential body of work than John Hughes' (2009). The *New York Times* reported that 'if auteur status is conferred by the possession of a recognizable style and set of themes, Mr. Hughes's place in the pantheon cannot be denied' (Scott 2009), while the Associated Press declared that 'Hughes defined not just a genre but a generation' (Lemire 2009). Alan Ruck, who played Cameron in *Ferris Bueller's Day Off* remarked that

> John was an American original. The reason he touched so many young people is that he treated his characters with dignity and respect and

not as objects of derision. The teenagers in John's stories are compassionate, adventurous, frustrated, loving, selfish, foolish, ambitious, confused, scared, brave, outraged, silly, needy, jealous, inspired – the list could be as long as you'd care to make it. John's characters are complete and complex and compelling and full of contradictions. Just like all of us. John's films remind us that life is challenging and complicated and wonderful, no matter what one's age might be.

(quoted in Gora 2010: 308)

In an exceptionally rare step indicating Hughes's vast significance, in the Academy Award ceremony after his death, there was a special tribute to the filmmaker. Instead of a passing picture in the 'In Memoriam' gallery, actors who worked with Hughes – Matthew Broderick, Macaulay Culkin, Jon Cryer, Anthony Michael Hall, Judd Nelson, Molly Ringwald, and Ally Sheedy – were all on stage to present an extended commemoration of Hughes and his films, complete with clips and commentary describing how important he was.

The Breakfast Club legacy

The Breakfast Club played heavily in the remembrance of Hughes's contribution to filmmaking, with a version of the song 'Don't You (Forget About Me)' playing as the actors took the Oscars stage. In the obituaries, the film was singled out as well, with *Variety* stating that 'John Hughes' 1985 pic "The Breakfast Club," more than any other film, captured the teen zeitgeist of the 1980s' (Saperstein 2009b) and *Vanity Fair* affirming that 'as hoary as it sounds, *The Breakfast Club* spoke to a generation. The elements that grown-ups perceived as ponderous and risible were precisely what made the movie so real to teens' (Kamp 2010b). Hughes made more financially successful films, but the teen films, especially *The Breakfast Club*, are the ones for which he is most remembered and the ones that cemented his status.

All the praise does not mean there are no faults with his work, with the teen films with which he was most closely associated, or with *The Breakfast Club*, the film most often pointed to as his masterpiece. The criticisms – about the political issues left out of the film and the troubling social and cultural issues in it – are valid. But as pointed out in the *New York Times*, 'his films are fables, not documentaries' (Scott 2009). This was on purpose; films would be changed in test screenings to satisfy audiences, and Hughes was resolutely interested in making fairy tales, albeit ones based on realistic experiences. Fittingly, it is this very nature of the films as fables that shows how they can be seen as coming-of-age myths – these mythical tales are exactly the types of stories especially suited to comprising genres and the genre films that endure. Even *The Breakfast Club*'s simple premise helps keep it perennial. Teens in high school, regardless of the time, can identify somehow with the characters' situation.

Interestingly, while *The Breakfast Club* functions as myth, what it does specifically that keeps it alive is leave off the explicit happy ending. Audiences do not know what will happen when school starts again. All the eternal conflicts the film addresses about how teens brave the coming-of-age process and all the questions about how they will mature into adults are left hanging. Even though the questions remain, the film still ends on an upbeat note because of hope, and because of Bender's triumphant, rebellious fist pump (see Figure 5.1). At least for the moment and for the day, there was a breakthrough. The problems of stereotypes and conflicts remain, but maybe this story and this day helped open some eyes. Its therapeutic, cathartic nature meant these teens, and perhaps the youth audiences that identified with them, felt like someone was listening. As Thomas Schatz describes, a reason audiences keep going back to genre films is because they address enduring cultural problems that have no easy real-world solutions, but film can offer temporary resolutions such as these.

The film remains of its time and classic as well not just because of the teen perspective it takes, but also because it could be appreciated on multiple levels by people of different ages at different times, and audiences could learn from it as well. When Ringwald saw the film with her daughter, it opened frank discussions about parental pressure, and she was furthermore

Figure 5.1 The iconic freeze-frame fist pump.

able to empathize with some of the adults after seeing things from a new standpoint (Glass 2014). And in the provocatively titled article 'The Most Important Message of *The Breakfast Club* Is a Lie,' a psychologist remarks that 'we actually learned the lessons' of the film by trying to address the social problems of bullying, stereotyping, and the stigma of mental illness that it raises, and that even though there is more work to do, progress is being made, thanks in part to the film (Friedman 2015). Attesting to one of the many reasons *The Breakfast Club* continues to be relevant, it engenders viewers to change perspectives. Younger audiences can realize they are not alone in the way they think and feel, and older audiences can remember the importance, and limits, of the teens' viewpoints. The film opens up avenues for seeing the world differently.

While *The Breakfast Club* is an exemplary teen film, it is also a product of its specific era. It captured a moment, and in many ways is representative of it, but it does not stand in for every other teen film either of the period or of the genre. No one film can. Indeed, different types of teen films, ranging from large-scale epics to personal dramas, slasher horror to ribald comedy, are in favor at different times, but their essential elements, that of teens figuring out who they are and who they want to be, remain intact. What Hughes and *The Breakfast Club* did was help crystallize the form, tell teen stories from their perspective, and treat teens like people who matter. *The Breakfast Club* provides a quintessential example of what the genre could be and could do. That the film endures as a classic is because it both captures a singular time and is timeless, and because the characters are so relatable, no matter what age.

Bibliography

'1985: The Year in Music & Video' (1985) *Billboard*, 28 December, p T–32.

'1986: The Year in Music & Video' (1986) *Billboard*, 27 December, p Y–36.

'The '80s Soundtracks' (1989) *Billboard*, 23 December, p D-24.

Albert, D. (1985) 'Youth May Be Wasted on Young but Its Appeal Is Showbiz Asset If You Know What It Is,' *Variety*, 16 January, p 7.

Altman, R. (1984/2012) 'A Semantic/Syntactic Approach to Film Genre,' in B. K. Grant (ed) *Film Genre Reader IV*, Austin: University of Texas Press, pp 27–41.

Altman, R. (1999) *Film/Genre*, London: BFI Publishing.

Anderson, C. (1994) *Hollywood TV: The Studio System in the Fifties*, Austin: University of Texas Press.

Appelo, T. (1994) 'John Hughes' View from the Top,' *Entertainment Weekly*, online, 2 December, http://ew.com/article/1994/12/02/john-hughes-view-top/.

Austin, J. and M. N. Willard (1998) *Generations of Youth: Youth Cultures and History in Twentieth-Century America*, New York: New York University Press.

Barnhart, D. K. and A. A. Metcalf (1997) *America in So Many Words: Words That Have Shaped America*, Boston: Houghton Mifflin.

Barth, J. (1984) 'Kinks of Comedy,' *Film Comment*, June, pp 44–47.

Bierbaum, T. (1984) 'Paramount Expects B.O. Boost with Re-Release of "Footloose" Same Day Cassette Hits Market,' *Variety*, 1 September, p 3.

Bierbaum, T. (1985) '"Missing 2" Wins September Videocassette Sales Derby,' *Daily Variety*, 27 September, p 24.

Bing, J. (2003) 'Hughes Wields Big "Club" in New H'wood,' *Variety*, 24 February, p 8.

Blakemore, E. (2015) 'The Latchkey Generation: How Bad Was It?' *JSTOR Daily*, online, 9 November, https://daily.jstor.org/latchkey-generation-bad/.

Bleach, A. C. (2010) 'Postfeminist Cliques? Class, Postfeminism, and the Molly Ringwald-John Hughes Films,' *Cinema Journal*, 49.3, pp 22–44.

Blum, D. (1985) 'Hollywood's Brat Pack,' *New York*, 10 June, pp 39–47.

Borrelli, C. (2015) '"The Breakfast Club" 30 Years Later: Don't You Forget About Them,' *Chicago Tribune*, online, 17 February, www.chicagotribune.com/entertainment/movies/ct-the-breakfast-club-30th-anniversary-20150217-column.html.

'The Breakfast Club' (1985) *Variety*, 13 February, p 19.

'The Breakfast Club' (2018) *Box Office Mojo*, online, www.boxofficemojo.com/movies/?id=breakfastclub.htm.

Brickman, B. (2012) *New American Teenagers: The Lost Generation of Youth in 1970s Film*, New York: Continuum.

Byrge, D. (1985) '"The Breakfast Club": THR's 1985 Review,' *The Hollywood Reporter*, online, 13 February, www.hollywoodreporter.com/news/breakfast-club-thrs-1985-review-773357.

Byrne Fields, A. (2009) 'Sincerely, John Hughes,' online, 6 August, http://wellknowwhenwegetthere.blogspot.com/2009/08/sincerely-john-hughes.html.

Carter, B. (1991) 'Him Alone,' *New York Times*, online, 4 August, www.nytimes.com/1991/08/04/magazine/him-alone.html.

Cateforis, T. (2014) *Are We Not New Wave?: Modern Pop at the Turn of the 1980s*, Ann Arbor: University of Michigan Press.

Cawelti, J. G. (1979/1995) '*Chinatown* and Generic Transformation in Recent American Films,' in B. K. Grant (ed) *Film Genre Reader II*, Austin: University of Texas Press, pp 227–245.

Chaney, J. (2015) 'The Adult Sympathies of *The Breakfast Club*,' *The Dissolve*, online, 11 March, https://thedissolve.com/features/exposition/952-the-adult-sympathies-of-the-breakfast-club/.

Christgau, R. (1985) 'Christgau's Consumer Guide,' *The Village Voice*, online, 25 June, www.robertchristgau.com/xg/cg/cgv6-85.php.

Christie, T. A. (2012) *John Hughes and Eighties Cinema: Teenage Hopes and American Dreams*, Maidstone, Kent: Crescent Moon Publishing.

Clover, C. (1992) *Men, Women, and Chainsaws: Gender in the Modern Horror Film*, Princeton, NJ: Princeton University Press.

Considine, D. M. (1985) *The Cinema of Adolescence*, Jefferson, NC: McFarland.

Corliss, R. (1986) 'Well, Hello Molly!' *Time*, online, 26 May, http://content.time.com/time/magazine/article/0,9171,144177,00.html.

Coupland, D. (1991) *Generation X: Tales for an Accelerated Culture*, New York: St. Martin's Press.

Denisoff, R. S. and W. D. Romanowski (1991) *Risky Business: Rock in Film*, New Brunswick, NJ: Transaction Publishers.

De Vaney, A. (2002) 'Pretty in Pink? John Hughes Reinscribes Daddy's Girl in Homes and Schools,' in F. K. Gateward and M. Pomerance (eds) *Sugar, Spice, and Everything Nice: Cinemas of Girlhood*, Detroit: Wayne State University Press, pp 201–216.

Dimock, M. (2018) 'Defining Generations: Where Millennials End and Post-Millennials Begin,' *Pew Research Center*, online, 1 March, www.pewresearch.org/fact-tank/2018/03/01/defining-generations-where-millennials-end-and-post-millennials-begin/.

Doherty, T. (2002) *Teenagers and Teenpics: The Juvenilization of American Movies in the 1950s*, Philadelphia: Temple University Press.

Driscoll, C. (2011) *Teen Film: A Critical Introduction*, Oxford: Berg Publishers.

Ebert, R. (1984) 'John Hughes: When You're 16, You're More Serious than You'll Ever Be Again,' *RogerEbert.com*, online, 29 April, www.rogerebert.com/rogers-journal/john-hughes-when-youre-16-youre-more-serious-than-youll-ever-be-again.

Ebert, R. (1985) 'The Breakfast Club,' *Chicago Sun-Times*, online, 15 February, www.rogerebert.com/reviews/the-breakfast-club-1985.

Ebert, R. (1986) 'Ferris Bueller's Day Off,' *Chicago Sun-Times*, online, 11 June, www.rogerebert.com/reviews/ferris-buellers-day-off-1986.

Ebert, R. (2009) 'John Hughes: In Memory,' *RogerEbert.com*, online, 6 August, www.rogerebert.com/interviews/john-hughes-in-memory.

Entertainment Weekly Staff (2015) '50 Best High School Movies,' *Entertainment Weekly*, online, 28 August, http://ew.com/gallery/50-best-high-school-movies-0/.

Epstein, B. S. (1984) 'Music Video – The Hot New Way to Sell Hot New Movies,' *Boxoffice*, July, pp 12–17.

Erlewine, S. T. (2002) 'New Wave,' in V. Bogdanov, C. Woodstra and S. T. Erlewine (eds) *All Music Guide to Rock: The Definitive Guide to Rock, Pop, and Soul*, San Francisco: Backbeat Books, p 1338.

Erlewine, S. T. (no date) 'The Breakfast Club [Original Soundtrack] AllMusic Review,' *AllMusic*, www.allmusic.com/album/the-breakfast-club-mw0000193096.

Faludi, S. (1991) *Backlash: The Undeclared War Against American Women*, New York: Crown Publishers, Inc.

Felando, C. (2000) 'Youth Must Be Served,' in D. Desser and G. S. Jowett (eds) *Hollywood Goes Shopping*, Minneapolis, MN: University of Minnesota Press, pp 82–107.

Feuer, J. (1995) *Seeing Through the Eighties: Television and Reaganism*, Durham, NC: Duke University Press.

'For Your Consideration: *The Breakfast Club*' (1985) *Variety*, 5 November, pp 8–9.

Freeman, H. (2016) *Life Moves Pretty Fast: The Lessons We Learned from Eighties Movies (and Why We Don't Learn Them from Movies Anymore)*, New York: Simon and Schuster Paperbacks.

Friedman, M. (2015) 'The Most Important Message of the [sic] The Breakfast Club Is a Lie,' *Huffington Post*, online, 19 February, www.huffingtonpost.com/michael-friedman-phd/the-most-important-message-of-the-breakfast-club-is-a-lie_b_6716016.html.

Frook, J. E. (1992) 'WB, Hughes Crack Deal for "Peanuts,"' *Variety*, online, 15 November, https://variety.com/1992/film/news/wb-hughes-crack-deal-for-peanuts-100425/.

Gelmis, J. (1985/2015) '"The Breakfast Club" 1985 Review: Nothing You Haven't Heard Before,' *Newsday*, online, 25 March, www.newsday.com/entertainment/movies/the-breakfast-club-1985-review-nothing-you-haven-t-heard-before-1.10083648.

Glass, I. (2014) 'Is That What I Look Like?' *This American Life*, 526, online, 23 May, www.thisamericanlife.org/526/is-that-what-i-look-like.

Gold, R. (1985) 'February Youth Pics Not Pulling Biz, Sneak Previews Could Be Bane,' *Variety*, 27 February, p 3.

Goldberg, F. (1983) 'Hollywood's View of Research Depends on Just Who's Being Asked, What Methods Are Used,' *Variety*, 12 January, p 10.

Goldstein, P. (1987) 'John Hughes in the Pink at MCA,' *Los Angeles Times*, online, 1 March, http://articles.latimes.com/1987-03-01/entertainment/ca-6707_1_john-hughes.

Goldstein, P. (2008) 'John Hughes' Imprint Remains,' *Los Angeles Times*, online, 24 March, https://web.archive.org/web/20080329232148/www.latimes.com/entertainment/news/movies/la-et-goldstein25mar25,0,3535882.story.

Goodwin, A. (1992) *Dancing in the Distraction Factory: Music Television and Popular Culture*, Minneapolis: University of Minnesota Press.

Gora, S. (2010) *You Couldn't Ignore Me If You Tried: The Brat Pack, John Hughes, and Their Impact on a Generation*, New York: Three Rivers Press.

Grant, B. K. (2003) 'Introduction,' in B. K. Grant (ed) *Film Genre Reader III*, Austin: University of Texas Press, pp xv–xx.

Grimes, W. (2009) 'Ned Tanen, Movie Executive with a Taste for Youth Films, Dies at 77,' *New York Times*, online, 8 January, www.nytimes.com/2009/01/08/movies/08tanen.html.

Grossberg, L. (1986) 'Is There Rock after Punk?' *Critical Studies in Mass Communication*, 3.1, pp 50–74.

Guzmán, R. (2015) '"The Breakfast Club" Review: 30 Years Later, It's Impossible to Forget About Them,' *Newsday*, online, 23 March, www.newsday.com/entertainment/movies/the-breakfast-club-review-30-years-later-it-s-impossible-to-forget-about-them-1.10078155.

Hall, G. S. (1904) *Adolescence: Its Psychology and Its Relations to Physiology, Anthropology, Sociology, Sex, Crime, Religion and Education*, New York: D. Appleton and Company.

Hilmes, M. (2014) *Only Connect: A Cultural History of Broadcasting in the United States*, 4th edition, Boston: Wadsworth.

Honeycutt, K. (2015) *John Hughes: A Life in Film*, New York: Race Point Publishing.

Hopkins, K. L. (2015) 'Banished from "The Breakfast Club": Actress Recalls the Burn of Getting Cut from John Hughes' Film,' *The Hollywood Reporter*, online, 25 March, www.hollywoodreporter.com/news/banished-breakfast-club-actress-recalls-784188.

Hughes, J. (2008) 'Vacation '58/Forward '08,' *Zoetrope: All-Story*, 12.2.

Kael, P. (1985) 'The Breakfast Club,' in *5001 Nights at the Movies*, New York: Picador.

Kael, P. (1989) 'Mars,' in *Hooked*, New York: E.P. Dutton.

Kamp, D. (2010a) 'John Hughes's Actors on John Hughes,' *Vanity Fair*, online, March, www.vanityfair.com/hollywood/features/2010/03/actors-on-john-hughes-201003.

Kamp, D. (2010b) 'Sweet Bard of Youth,' *Vanity Fair*, online, March, www.vanityfair.com/hollywood/features/2010/03/john-hughes-201003.

Kamp, D. (2018) '*The Breakfast Club*: Smells Like Teen Realness,' *The Breakfast Club: Criterion Collection*, www.criterion.com/current/posts/5243-the-breakfast-club-smells-like-teen-realness.

Kelly, M. (2001) 'John Hughes: The Films He Created in the Decade of Greed Made Adolescent Angst Funny and Bearable without Romanticizing It,' *Salon*, online, 17 July, www.salon.com/2001/07/17/john_hughes_2/.

Klein, A. A. (2011) *American Film Cycles: Reframing Genres, Screening Social Problems, & Defining Subcultures*, Austin: University of Texas Press.

Kreps, D. (2016) '"Breakfast Club," "Rushmore" Among Films Added to National Film Registry,' *Rolling Stone*, online, 14 December, www.rollingstone.com/movies/movie-news/breakfast-club-rushmore-among-films-added-to-national-film-registry-124616/.

Lallch, R. (1993) 'Big Baby,' *Spy*, January, pp 66–77.

Lemire, C. (2009) 'John Hughes Defined a Genre and a Generation,' Associated Press, online, 6 August, https://newsok.com/article/feed/65269/john-hughes-defined-a-genre-and-a-generation.

Lévi-Strauss, C. (1963) *Structural Anthropology*, translated by C. Jacobson and B. G. Schoepf, New York: Basic Books, Inc.

Litwak, M. (1986) *Reel Power: The Struggle for Influence and Success in the New Hollywood*, New York: New American Library.

'Local Election Ratings Topped by KTLA's Club' (1988) *Variety*, 10 November, p 22.

Mannheim, K. (1952/1968) *Essays on the Sociology of Knowledge*, edited by P. Kecskemeti, London: Routledge.

Manzoor, S. (2004) 'More than a Quintessential Eighties Teen Film,' *The Independent*, online, 24 March, www.independent.co.uk/arts-entertainment/films/features/more-than-a-quintessential-eighties-teen-film-65704.html.

Martens, T. (2009) 'John Hughes: The Soundtrack to a Generation,' *Pop & Hiss: The L.A. Times Music Blog*, online, 6 August, http://latimesblogs.latimes.com/music_blog/2009/08/john-hughes-the-music.html.

Maslin, J. (1985) 'John Hughes's "Breakfast Club,"' *New York Times*, online, 15 February, www.nytimes.com/movie/review?res=9C0CE0D61439F936A257 51C0A963948260.

Maslin, J. (1987) 'Film View; Marching toward Maturity,' *New York Times*, online, 15 March, p 21.

MPA (Motion Picture Association) (1990) 'U.S. Economic Review,' online, http://mpaa.org/.

MPAA (Motion Picture Association of America) (no date) '2000: U.S. Economic Review,' online, http://mpaa.org/.

Mullen, M. (2003) *The Rise of Cable Programming in the United States: Revolution or Evolution?* Austin: University of Texas Press.

Nelson, E. H. (2011) *Teen Films of the 1980s: Genre, New Hollywood, and Generation X*, Unpublished PhD Thesis, University of Texas at Austin.

Nelson, E. H. (2017) 'The New Old Face of a Genre: The Franchise Teen Film as Industry Strategy,' *Cinema Journal*, 57.1, pp 125–133.

O'Connor, T. (1986) 'John Hughes: His Movies Speak to Teen-Agers,' *New York Times*, online, 9 March, www.nytimes.com/1986/03/09/movies/john-hughes-his-movies-speak-to-teen-agers.html.

O'Toole, K. (1998) 'It's Not Only Generation X: Malaise, Cynicism on Rise for All,' *Stanford Report*, online, 26 August, https://news.stanford.edu/news/1998/august26/genx.html.

Owen, R. (1997) *Gen X TV: The Brady Bunch to Melrose Place*, Syracuse, NY: Syracuse University Press.

'Picks and Pans Review: The Breakfast Club' (1985) *People*, online, 18 February, https://people.com/archive/picks-and-pans-review-the-breakfast-club-vol-23-no-7/.

Prince, S. (2000) *A New Pot of Gold: Hollywood under the Electronic Rainbow, 1980–1989*, Berkeley: University of California Press.

'Readers' Poll: The Top 25 Greatest Movies of the 1980s' (2014) *Rolling Stone*, online, 19 February, www.rollingstone.com/music/pictures/readers-poll-the-25-greatest-movies-of-the-1980s-20140219.

Rettenmund, M. (1996) *Totally Awesome 80s: A Lexicon of the Music, Videos, Movies, TV Shows, Stars, and Trends of That Decadent Decade*, New York: St. Martin's Griffin.

Ringwald, M. (1986) 'Molly Ringwald Interviews John Hughes,' *Seventeen*, March, pp 226–228 and 238–240.

Ringwald, M. (2009) 'The Neverland Club,' *New York Times*, online, 12 August, www.nytimes.com/2009/08/12/opinion/12ringwald.html.

Ringwald, M. (2018) 'What About "The Breakfast Club"?: Revisiting the Movies of My Youth in the Age of #MeToo,' *The New Yorker*, 6 April, www.newyorker.com/culture/personal-history/what-about-the-breakfast-club-molly-ringwald-metoo-john-hughes-pretty-in-pink.

Roberts, S. (2016) 'A Diamond and a Kiss: The Women of John Hughes,' *Hazlitt*, online, 5 July, http://hazlitt.net/longreads/diamond-and-kiss-women-john-hughes.

Roth, M. (1986) 'Teens Leaving Theaters for Homevid, New Study Gives Exhibs Bad News,' *Variety*, 26 February, p 3.

Rottenberg, J. (2009) 'John Hughes Remembered,' *Entertainment Weekly*, 14 August, pp 26–31.

Saperstein, P. (2009a) 'Director John Hughes Dies at 59,' *Variety*, August 6, https://variety.com/2009/film/markets-festivals/director-john-hughes-dies-at-59-1118006975/.

Saperstein, P. (2009b) 'Studio Exec Ned Tanen Dies at 77,' *Variety*, online, 5 January, http://variety.com/2009/film/features/studio-exec-ned-tanen-dies-at-77-1117997962/.

Schatz, T. G. (1981) *Hollywood Genres: Formulas, Filmmaking, and the Studio System*, New York: Random House.

Schatz, T. G. (1993) 'The New Hollywood,' in J. Collins, H. Radner and A. Preacher Collins (eds) *Film Theory Goes to the Movies*, New York: Routledge, pp 1–36.

Schneller, J. (2007) 'Channeling the Eighties,' *Globe and Mail*, online, 9 March, www.theglobeandmail.com/arts/channelling-the-eighties/article20394218/.

Schuman, H. and W. L. Rogers (2004) 'Cohorts, Chronology, and Collective Memories,' *Public Opinion Quarterly*, 68.2, pp 217–254.

Scott, A. O. (2009) 'An Appraisal: The John Hughes Touch,' *New York Times*, online, 8 August, www.nytimes.com/2009/08/08/movies/08appraisal.html?fta=y.

Scott, J. (1983) 'The Wild Ones,' *American Film*, April, pp 30–35 and 64–65.

Shary, T. (2002) *Generation Multiplex: The Image of Youth in Contemporary American Cinema*, Austin: University of Texas Press.

Sheedy, A. (2007) 'Forward,' in Jaime Clarke (ed) *Don't You Forget About Me: Contemporary Writers on the Films of John Hughes*, New York: Simon Spotlight Entertainment, pp xi–xiii.

Siskel, G. (1985a) 'Teenage Life Gets a Touching New Portrayal,' *Chicago Tribune*, online, 15 February, http://articles.chicagotribune.com/1985-02-15/entertainment/8501090715_1_breakfast-club-sixteen-candles-film.

Siskel, G. (1985b) 'John Huhges Wakes Up to Needs of Teens with "Breakfast Club,"' *Chicago Tribune*, online, 17 February, http://articles.chicagotribune.com/1985-02-17/entertainment/8501090893_1_sixteen-candles-writer-director-john-hughes-film.

Sklar, R. (1994) *Movie-Made America: A Cultural History of American Movies, Revised and Updated*, New York: Vintage Books.

Smith, F. (2017) *Rethinking the Hollywood Teen Movie: Gender, Genre and Identity*, Edinburgh: Edinburgh University Press.

Smith, J. (1998) *The Sounds of Commerce: Marketing Popular Film Music*, New York: Columbia University Press.

Smith, S. M. (1999) 'Teen Days That Shook the World,' *Premiere*, December, pp 69–79 and 145–146.

Stam, R. (2000) *Film Theory: An Introduction*, Malden, MA: Blackwell Publishers.

Strauss, W. and N. Howe (1991) *Generations: The History of America's Future, 1584 to 2069*, New York: William Morrow and Company, Inc.

Thompson, K. and D. Bordwell (2010) *Film History: An Introduction*, Boston, MA: McGraw Hill.

'Top DVD Sales' (2003) *Billboard*, 3 May, p 51.

Tropiano, S. (2006) *Rebels and Chicks: A History of the Hollywood Teen Movie*, New York: Back Stage Books.

Tusher, W. (1985) 'John Hughes Signs Feature Deal with Par,' *Daily Variety*, 22 March.

Tyson, L. (2015) *Critical Theory Today: A User-Friendly Guide*, 3rd edition, New York: Routledge.

'United States' (2007) in T. L. Gall (ed) *Worldmark Encyclopedia of the States*, 7th edition, vol. 2, Detroit: Gale, pp 993–1050.

Valenti, J. (1985) 'Admissions by Age Groups 1982–84,' *Variety*, 16 January, p 94.

Van Tuyl, L. (1989) 'Fewer Teens, but They Spend More,' *Christian Science Monitor*, 14 March, p 14.

Vogler, C. (2007) *The Writer's Journey: Mythic Structure for Writers*, 3rd edition, Studio City, CA: Michael Wiese Productions.

Wasko, J. (1994) *Hollywood in the Information Age: Beyond the Silver Screen*, Austin: University of Texas Press.

Wasser, F. (2001) *Veni, Vidi, Video: The Hollywood Empire and the VCR*, Austin: University of Texas Press.

Weiss, M. (2006) 'Some Kind of Republican,' *Slate*, online, 21 September, www.slate.com/articles/arts/dvdextras/2006/09/some_kind_of_republican.html.

Wood, J. (2015) 'Don't You Forget About Me: "Breakfast Club" at 30,' *Rolling Stone*, online, 24 February, www.rollingstone.com/culture/culture-lists/dont-you-forget-about-me-breakfast-club-at-30-141934/john-green-author-the-fault-in-our-stars-186676/.

Wood, R. (1977/2012) 'Ideology, Genre, Auteur,' in B. K. Grant (ed) *Film Genre Reader II*, Austin: University of Texas Press, pp 78–92.

Wright, W. (1975) *Six Guns and Society: A Structural Study of the Western*, Berkeley: University of California Press.

Wyatt, J. (1994) *High Concept: Movies and Marketing in Hollywood*, Austin: University of Texas Press.

'Youth Barometer Tracks Patterns of Entertainment Habits, Spending' (1985) *Variety*, 13 February, p 2.

Index

Note: page numbers in italics indicate a figure on the corresponding pages.